D0472258

the **Ab●ut**.com guide to

ACOUSTIC GUITAR

Step-by-Step Instruction to Start Playing Today

Dan Cross with Douglas Lichterman

Adams Media
Avon, Massachusetts

About About.com

About.com is a powerful network of 500 Guides—smart, passionate, accomplished people who are experts in their fields. About.com Guides live and work in more than twenty countries and celebrate their interests in thousands of topics. They have written books, appeared on national television programs, and won many awards in their fields. Guides are selected for their ability to provide the most interesting information for users, and for their passion for their subject and the Web. The selection process is rigorous—only 15 percent of those who apply actually become Guides. The following are some of the most important criteria by which they are chosen:

- High level of knowledge/passion for their topic
- Appropriate credentials
- Keen understanding of the Web experience
- Commitment to creating informative, actionable features

Each month more than 48 million people visit About.com. Whether you need home repair and decorating ideas, recipes, movie trailers, or car buying tips, About.com Guides can offer practical advice and solutions for everyday life. Wherever you land on About.com, you'll always find content that is relevant to your interests. If you're looking for "how to" advice on refinishing your deck, About.com will also show you the tools you need to get the job done. No matter where you are on About.com, or how you got there, you'll always find exactly what you're looking for!

About Your Guide

 DAN CROSS is a professional guitarist and private instructor living in New York City. He received his formal music education at Humber College in Toronto, Ontario and the Mohawk College Jazz Studies program in Hamilton, Ontario, from which he graduated with honors.

Dan has performed professionally throughout the United States and Canada, in addition to touring with a jazz band in Europe and performing at the prestigious Montreux Jazz Festival. He has also scored music for Canadian television shows.

Dan has ten years of experience as a guitar teacher. "Teaching is in my blood, and I enjoy helping others further their guitar knowledge," he says. "I'm an avid music fan with a keen interest in all types of music, including pop, jazz, classic rock—even German beer jingles." The wide assortment of interests his students bring keeps Dan on top of all the current trends in music and guitar.

Acknowledgments

Thanks to my parents, for helping to support me when my playing/teaching wasn't paying the rent; to my wife, for coming to accept that keeping five guitars in a New York apartment isn't excessive; and to Douglas, for crafting my incoherent ramblings into a finely crafted lesson structure.

ABOUT.COM

CEO & President
Scott Meyer

COO
Andrew Pancer

SVP Content
Michael Daecher

VP Marketing
Lisa Abourezk

Director, About Operations
Chris Murphy

Senior Web Designer
Jason Napolitano

ADAMS MEDIA

Editorial

Publishing Director
Gary M. Krebs

Associate Managing Editor
Laura M. Daly

Development Editor
Katie McDonough

Marketing

Director of Marketing
Karen Cooper

Assistant Art Director
Frank Rivera

Production

Director of Manufacturing
Susan Beale

Associate Director of Production
Michelle Roy Kelly

Senior Book Designer
Colleen Cunningham

Published by Adams Media, an F+W Publications Company
57 Littlefield Street
Avon, MA 02322
www.adamsmedia.com

ISBN 10: 1-59869-098-1
ISBN 13: 978-1-59869-098-9

Printed in China.

J I H G F E D C B A

Library of Congress Cataloging-in-Publication Data is available from the publisher.

This publication is designed to provide accurate and authoritative information with regard to the subject matter covered. It is sold with the understanding that the publisher is not engaged in rendering legal, accounting, or other professional advice. If legal advice or other expert assistance is required, the services of a competent professional person should be sought.

—From a *Declaration of Principles* jointly adopted by a Committee of the American Bar Association and a Committee of Publishers and Associations

Many of the designations used by manufacturers and sellers to distinguish their product are claimed as trademarks. Where those designations appear in this book and Adams Media was aware of a trademark claim, the designations have been printed with initial capital letters.

Some of the Web sites referenced in this book may show copyrighted music and lyrics. This information is intended only for private study, scholarship, or research.

Line art provided by Dan Cross.

This book is available at quantity discounts for bulk purchases.
For information, please call 1-800-872-5627.

How to Use This Book

Each About.com book is written by an About.com Guide—an expert with experiential knowledge of his or her subject. While the book can stand on its own as a helpful resource, it can also be coupled with the corresponding About.com site for even more tips, tools, and advice to help you learn even more about a particular subject. Each book will not only refer you back to About .com, but it will also direct you to other useful Internet locations and print resources.

All About.com books include a special section at the end of each chapter called Get Linked. Here you'll find a few links back to the About.com site for even more great information on the topics discussed in that chapter. Depending on the topic, these could be links to such resources as photos, sheet music, quizzes, recipes, or product reviews.

About.com books also include four types of sidebars:

- **Ask Your Guide:** Detailed information in a question-and-answer format
- **Tools You Need:** Advice about researching, purchasing, and using a variety of tools for your projects
- **Elsewhere on the Web:** References to other useful Internet locations
- **What's Hot:** All you need to know about the hottest trends and tips out there

Each About.com book will take you on a personal tour of a certain topic, give you reliable advice, and leave you with the knowledge you need to achieve your goals.

CONTENTS

CONTENTS . . . *continued*

Introduction from Your Guide

Every guitarist remembers the moment when he or she first caught the spark. It might have been seeing a friend or family member play the guitar, or hearing a particular song on the radio, or attending a concert where a guitarist gave a hot performance, or having your eye caught by a window full of guitars at a music store. Whatever that moment was for you, it ignited something inside and struck you with head-slapping certainty—you knew you wanted to play the guitar! Welcome to the club.

Learning to play the guitar well is a journey with a million little steps. Before you even strum your first chord you'll want to learn the parts of your instrument (so you can talk knowledgeably with other guitarists), learn how to hold the guitar correctly, how to tune it, what the names of the strings are, how to hold your pick. Once you do start to strum that first chord you'll want to hit just the right strings with the right amount of force. And when you fret the notes of the chord you'll want each note to ring out clearly. Then you'll want to be able to switch quickly from one chord to another. Each little step paves the way to understanding the next step on your path to learning to play the guitar.

It sounds like a lot of work, and it is, but the guitar is an inviting instrument and it hooks you quickly. With just a lesson or two you can learn enough basic chords and strums to play your guitar in a way that's very rewarding, and the energy you get from your early success will fuel your efforts to study harder, get better, and learn more.

The acoustic guitar is the purest form of the instrument. The vibration of the strings is transmitted through the bridge to the body of the guitar, which then vibrates itself, projecting the sound out through the sound hole. It's loud enough to fill a room, which has made the guitar the most popular instrument for blues, folk, and country players for decades. Your acoustic guitar is portable—it can travel along with you, bringing its rich, vibrant sound anywhere you need it.

More than that, your guitar can be a conduit for your artistic expression, both as the "voice" of your playing and as a tool for creating your own compositions. As such, you'll find that you develop a close relationship with your guitar. You won't want to leave it behind. It can be your best friend during hard times.

The guitar has a rich history, going back hundreds of years. In this book we'll focus on the instrument as it has existed in the twentieth century and into the twenty-first, looking to some of the musicians who led the development of the guitar in the classical, blues, folk, pop, and rock genres for our inspiration.

This book is designed to be a companion to my guitar Web site on About.com. You can find my site at http://guitar.about.com. Many times I'll refer you to various locations on the Web site where you can listen to examples of the riffs, scales, chords, or strumming patterns we're studying. At other times I'll send you to areas on my Web site where you can further study subjects that we can only touch upon here. I hope the site will become a familiar clubhouse for you, a place where you can come to relax and immerse yourself in the instrument we've all come to love.

It's exciting that you've decided to learn to play, and I'm honored that you've chosen me to be your guide to the acoustic guitar. We're going to have a lot of fun together.

Chapter 1

Getting Started

First Things First: Getting a Guitar

Once you've decided you want to learn to play acoustic guitar, the first thing you're going to need is an instrument to practice on. If you don't already have a guitar, there are three ways to get one—buy it, rent it, or borrow it.

If you're already pretty sure guitar is for you, buying an instrument is your best option. The design and workmanship of inexpensive guitars has improved dramatically over the past couple of decades, so there are a lot of great beginner instruments under $300.

Renting a guitar has the advantage of not having to lay out a lot of money at once, and if you "rent to own," a part of your rental payments will apply to the purchase of your instrument. Generally, renting a beginner instrument costs $5–$10 per week, and the rental is usually offered in blocks of several weeks at a time. The down side of renting is that all or a lot of the money you put in just goes away with no instrument to show for it, so try not to spend more than $100 renting before you buy a guitar.

About

If you have a friend or relative who has a guitar that he or she isn't using, or a collection of guitars, you might be able to borrow your first instrument. If you do borrow, be sensitive to how soon your friend or family member wants the instrument back, and take care to keep it clean and protected from harm.

Acoustic guitars come in many shapes and sizes. Luckily, all these choices break down into just a few categories. The most commonly used acoustic guitar is the 6-string with steel strings—**6-string steel**—which some people refer to as a **folk guitar**. These instruments have a bright, powerful ringing tone because of the steel strings and the large wooden bodies, which project the sound.

Acoustic steel-string guitars also come in a **12-string** version, which uses two strings where each string would normally be. The pairs of strings are tuned an octave apart or to exactly the same pitch, to double the sound of each string. These guitars have a rich sound that's distinctive (think songs such as "Turn, Turn, Turn" by the Byrds or "Stairway to Heaven" by Led Zeppelin). They're harder to tune and play than the 6-string version, but the sound can be addicting.

The **6-string classical** guitar is also known as a **nylon-string** because its strings are made of nylon. The treble (higher-pitched) strings are clear, white, or black in color and feel like plastic, while the bass strings have metallic binding wrapped around them, which makes them look like steel strings. These guitars have a softer, mellower sound than steel-string instruments. Some beginners like classical guitars better because the nylon strings feel softer than steel strings and are easier to press down, which allows you to play longer before your fingers start to hurt—especially before you've developed calluses on the end of the fingers on your fretting hand (the one that presses the strings against the neck). But classical guitars also have wider necks, which makes reaching all the strings a little harder. Classical guitars also come in a 12-string variety.

Acoustic guitars that have a pickup built in so they can be amplified are known as **acoustic/electric** guitars. They sound like acoustic guitars when they aren't plugged into an amplifier, and when they are plugged in they can be very loud and can also be put through effects, which are electronic devices that alter your sound in various ways.

A **resonator guitar** is an acoustic guitar that has a metal resonator built into the body. This system was invented to make guitars louder—and it does—but with the invention of the guitar amplifier this function became unnecessary. A resonator guitar can easily be identified by the large steel plate on the front surrounding the bridge, and it usually has two additional sound holes, sometimes covered with metal screens, on either side of the neck on the face. The bridge of the instrument is connected directly to the resonator, which when vibrating acts like a speaker cone and makes the sound louder, with a tone that's almost banjo-like. These guitars are usually played with a slide and with the instrument lying flat on your lap. They can also be played like a regular acoustic guitar.

Different Styles, Different Instruments

The kind of acoustic guitar you'll want to buy depends a lot on the kind of music you want to play. Here are some styles of playing and the best guitar(s) to play them on:

- **Rock/Alternative rock:** 6-string steel, 12-string steel
- **Funk:** 6-string steel
- **Folk:** 6-string steel, 12-string steel, classical
- **Fingerpicking style:** 6-string steel, 12-string steel, classical
- **Blues:** 6-string steel, 12-string steel, resonator
- **Jazz:** 6-string steel, 12-string steel, classical
- **Brazilian:** classical
- **Flamenco:** classical
- **Bluegrass:** 6-string steel, 12-string steel, resonator

ELSEWHERE ON THE WEB

▶ The 12-string is used much less commonly than the 6-string, but it does have a devoted following of excellent guitarists. If you're trying to figure out whether 12-string is for you, check out this excellent article, which appeared in *Acoustic Guitar* magazine. It details the history of the instrument and some of the great musicians who made it popular, from the earliest blues players to rockers of today. Just go to www.frets.com/FRETSPages/History/12string/12stOrigins.html.

- **Flatpicking style:** 6-string steel
- **Country:** 6-string steel, 12-string steel
- **Classical:** classical
- **Slide:** 6-string steel, resonator

Where to Buy or Not to Buy Your Guitar

Choosing a beginner instrument can be tricky, since the chances are you don't know a whole lot about guitars to begin with. It's best if you go somewhere that has a lot of different guitars you can check out, as well as experienced salespeople who can help you. If you live in a metropolitan area there's probably a Guitar Center, Sam Ash Music, or another national music store chain outlet nearby that will have the largest selection in town, and possibly the lowest prices. Be sure to check your local instrument stores too—in many cases these mom-and-pop stores will give you the most personalized service and attention as you search for your new guitar.

It's also best to avoid buying your first guitar from online music stores or auction sites such as eBay, because you can't see, feel, or hear the actual instrument before you make your purchase. Keep these online options in mind for when you know more about guitars, though, because they often do have great deals and hard-to-find instruments you might be searching for.

Fifteen Great Instruments for Beginners

This section describes fifteen low-cost instruments that provide outstanding value for the price. Please note that the prices shown are approximations of the prices found in stores and online as of this book's publication, and they can vary or change at any time.

6-string steel These 6-string steel acoustic guitars are great starter instruments for those who want to play the type of guitar that sets the standard for the steel-string family.

- **Epiphone DR-100:** This instrument features a spruce top, with mahogany back and sides. This guitar can usually be found at a rather cheap price, which makes it attractive to beginners. Most consider this a strictly beginner instrument, however, so it may not be long before you'll want to trade up. $130.
- **Fender DG-8S:** This is an excellent value for an inexpensive instrument. It's a natural-finish **dreadnought** with a solid spruce top that feels great in your hands. At the time of this writing the DG-8S is being offered as a package deal that includes a chromatic tuner, gig bag, shoulder strap, picks, guitar strings, string winder, and an instructional DVD. $200.
- **Washburn D10S:** This was named the number one guitar under $500 by *Acoustic Guitar* magazine—and it only costs $200! Small wonder that this instrument is the world's best-selling acoustic guitar. It has a solid spruce top with mahogany back and sides, a **nato** neck with a **sonokelin** fingerboard, and smooth Grover-style tuners. A great value! $200.
- **Takamine GS-330S:** This guitar looks and feels as good as instruments that cost twice as much. It has a solid cedar top with nato back and sides, a mahogany neck, and a rosewood fingerboard and bridge. The natural finish feels great in your hands, and the sound is bright and strong. $299.
- **Blueridge BR-40:** This guitar offers some of the best craftsmanship available on a guitar of its price. It has a solid spruce top with mahogany back and sides, and a mahogany neck with rosewood fingerboard and a rosewood bridge. The attention to detail is evident in the five-ply body binding and the beautiful mother-of-pearl inlay work on the tuning head, and the old-fashioned tuning pegs add a timeless look. Sounds like a much more expensive instrument. $300.
- **Ibanez AC110NT:** This is a natural-finish instrument that has a solid spruce top with walnut sides and back. This

ASK YOUR GUIDE

Are there different size options for younger people, whose hands are still growing, or for adults with small hands?

▸ Yes. If you have smaller hands, you might be more comfortable playing a smaller instrument. Besides full size, guitars also come in ½ size and ¾ size versions with shorter necks (which means less finger stretching) and smaller bodies, which are easier to reach around. Both steel-string and nylon-string guitars come in these sizes.

combination gives the guitar a rich, warm bottom-end sound with bright highs on top. $345.

- **Seagull S6:** These Canadian-made instruments are terrific guitars—highly regarded, both for their beautiful sound and their excellent value. The S6 features a solid cedar top with mahogany back and sides. Although the price may be slightly above what some might be willing to pay for a first guitar, it should be considered an investment. $360.

¾ **size 6-string steel** instruments offer the same craftsmanship and attention to detail as their bigger sisters in a size that comfortably accommodates anyone with smaller hands. They also make good traveling guitars when space is an issue.

- **Taylor Baby Taylor:** The Taylor Baby Taylor is a great-sounding ¾ size dreadnought from one of the top American guitar makers. This purebred puppy has a solid spruce top with sapele laminate back and sides, a mahogany neck with ebony fretboard, and an ebony bridge. The two screws in the fretboard on the sixteenth fret are a little startling, but they don't affect the sound of the instrument. Also comes in a Mahogany Top version. Gig bag included. $270.
- **Martin LXI:** The Martin LXI, one of the "Little Martin" line, is proof that even Martins can be affordable—if you make them small! This ¾ size guitar by the legendary American maker has a solid spruce top with mahogany pattern HPL back and sides, a Stratabond neck with Micarta fingerboard, and a Micarta bridge. Is it a high-quality instrument with a good sound? It's a Martin—enough said. Gig bag included. $280.
- **Washburn WD9SW ¾ Size:** The Washburn WD9SW is a ¾ size guitar that makes a very fine instrument for a young beginner with small hands, or for an adult who prefers a

smaller guitar. The top is solid sapele, as are the back and sides, with a mahogany neck and an ebony fingerboard. Grover tuners help it sound as pretty as it looks. $300.

12-string steel These 12-strings stand out for their shimmering sound and solid construction. Their excellent playability makes them a good choice for starting out if 12-string is going to be your thing.

- **Washburn D10S-12 12-string:** This is the 12-string sister of the bestselling D10S. It has a solid spruce top with mahogany back and sides, a mahogany neck with rosewood fingerboard, and a rosewood bridge. The action is low, making it a breeze to play, and it sounds sweet. $255.
- **Yamaha FG720S-12 12-String:** This is an elegant instrument with a clear, crisp sound. It has a solid spruce top with nato sides and back, a rosewood fingerboard, and a rosewood bridge. Nice low action makes it a pleasure to play. $330.

Classical / nylon-string Both of these classical guitars bring the timeless sound of nylon-stringed instruments into the reach of beginners. Here's a tip: Using "high tension" nylon strings gives you the stability of steel strings with the roundness of the nylon sound.

- **Yamaha CG-111S:** This is a nicely crafted classical guitar for a reasonable price. It has a solid spruce top with nato back and sides, a nato neck with rosewood fingerboard, and a rosewood bridge. This instrument has a nice feel and a rich, round tone. $230.
- **Alvarez Artist Series AC60S:** This nylon-string guitar has a solid cedar top with mahogany back and sides, a rosewood fingerboard, and a rosewood bridge. It's a well-crafted instrument with a natural gloss finish and a rich sound. $280.

Resonator

- **Fender FR-50 Resonator:** This resonator guitar comes set up nicely for playing like a regular acoustic guitar, with low action, a round neck (some are square and meant for playing lap slide) and a nice, if mild, version of the classic resonator sound. It has a spruce top with mahogany back and sides, a round nato neck with rosewood fingerboard, and F-holes in the shape of the classic Fender "F." $350.

Getting the Best from the Guitar Store

For many guitarists, especially novices, trying out a guitar in a music store can be an intimidating experience. Invariably, there are several other guitarists in the store who feel the need to show off their skills on the instrument, by playing all their most impressive licks. The first few times I tried out a guitar in a music store, I remember playing very quietly so no one would hear that I wasn't very good. This is a perfectly natural instinct, but in retrospect, I've realized it was the silliest thing I could have done. In order to really hear the tonal qualities of an acoustic guitar, you need to play it at a reasonable volume, so don't be afraid to strum the open strings hard, listening to the guitar's sustain and keeping an ear open for problems, such as buzzing strings. If you're having a hard time hearing (due to other guitarists in the store, conversation, and so on), ask if you can try the guitar in a separate room, or in a quieter part of the store. If the salespeople aren't willing to help you with that, feel free to thank them and take your business to a better store.

Focus on your primary goal. You want to find the best instrument possible for the least money. The reality is that you want to find the best guitar at the top of your price range, and then get *that* instrument for the lowest possible price. Avoid buying an ultra-cheap instrument, because it will be frustratingly hard to play and keep in tune, which will only make learning to play more difficult.

It's important to remember that, as the customer, you're the one who's in charge. Don't let the salespeople intimidate you, and remember that you don't have to buy any guitar you have doubts about. On the other hand, it's great to get your salesperson on your side by asking for his or her advice. Most salespeople in guitar stores are guitarists themselves, so they'll be happy to provide their point of view about which guitars in your price range are the most playable. Make it a case of you and the salesperson teaming up to find the best guitar possible.

You don't have to buy a guitar during this visit to the store—in fact, it's better to plan *not* to buy one on your first trip. Instead, take the time to try out many instruments. Make notes about every guitar you like, writing down the manufacturer, the model number, the price, and what you liked about the guitar. Then go home and do some further research on the instruments you are trying to decide among. (I'll tell you how to do that later in this chapter.)

If you have friends or relatives who know more about guitars than you do, bring them along—the more people who care about your finding a great instrument, the better!

Look at all the instruments in your price range until you find one that appeals to you. Then ask a salesperson to take it down for you, or take it down yourself if it's allowed. A word of caution—acoustic guitars are delicate, and they're usually hung close together in stores, so be very careful when taking down guitars or putting them back on their hooks, because if you bang them together the salespeople will have plenty to say about it!

Here's what to check for when trying out a guitar:

- **Sound/tone:** When strummed, strings should sound bright and clear with good sustain.

▶ Every guitarist needs what are referred to as basic guitar tools. These include a wire cutter, for cutting the loose ends off strings when you change them, and an Allen wrench, for adjusting the truss rod inside your guitar neck when necessary. There are all-purpose tools, such as the Roadie Rench, that combine all the guitar tools you'll need into one handle.

- **Action:** The term action describes how high the strings rest above the neck. "Good action" means the strings are as close to the neck as possible without buzzing against the frets (not more than ⅛ inch above the fret at the 12th fret).
- **Good intonation:** This means that the fretted notes are in tune all up and down the neck. The first check is that the harmonic above the twelfth fret matches the fretted note on the twelfth fret. If they're different, it means there's an intonation problem with the neck or bridge.
- **No buzzing:** Play every note on every string to make sure the notes are clear and not buzzing. (Buzzing occurs when the string is too close to a fret.)
- **Stays in tune:** Once tuned, the instrument should remain in tune for as long as you're trying it.
- **Has good tuning machines:** Tune each string a little—the tuning machines should feel smooth and the pitch should go up and down fluidly, with no catching or "tink" sounds.

Do your research. Once you've been to the guitar store and selected a few possibilities, your next step should be to go online and look up the manufacturers' Web sites, where you can find additional information about specifications and warranties on the instruments you're considering (see the Get Linked section at the end of this chapter for a link about brands of guitars).

Step two is to find out what other guitar players think about the instruments you're considering. Take note of the prices people paid for their guitars, and pay close attention to any problems they mention so you can check them out for yourself the next time you play that instrument. (See the Get Linked section at the end of this chapter for the Gear Reviews Archive links resource.) Another good place for guitarist feedback about instruments is the About .com Guitar Forum, where you can not only read reviews, but also post questions about the exact guitars you're considering, such as "Anybody played the Ibanez AW40?" Chances are good that you'll get some quick responses from the guitar community.

Step three is to look up the phone numbers of any other music stores in your area and give each of them a call to see if they carry any of the guitars you're considering. You'll have to tell them the name of the manufacturer and the exact model number for each guitar, such as "Epiphone DR-100." If one of the stores has any of them, ask the salesperson to quote you the price. You might encounter some resistance to this request because (A) they don't want to quote prices to the competition, and (B) they want you to come in to the store so they have a shot at selling you a guitar. However, if you mention that you're about to buy a guitar at *another store*, salespeople become much more forthcoming! Keep notes of the differences in price for each guitar on your list.

Now that you've amassed all this research, and ideally have narrowed your list down to one favorite instrument, it's time for the final phase—the fateful trip to the music store that will end with you bringing home your new guitar!

You've picked your instrument. Now your mission is to bring that baby home for the lowest possible price! Note that this changes your relationship with your salesperson from teammate to adversary, because his or her mission is to sell it to you for as much money as possible. Your mantra will be "*never* pay list price." Say it again. Many people assume that if the price tag on the guitar says $599, that's the price they'll be expected to pay. This is not true—music stores *expect* to sell you the guitar for less than list price. Many stores show both the list price and their own price on the tag in an effort to impress you in advance with the discount you'll be getting. Whatever the price tag says, remember that your salesperson has the power to significantly reduce the price of your

What's a harmonic?

▶ On certain frets it's possible to just barely touch the string as you pluck it and elicit a little bell tone. Just lift your finger off the string at the same time that you pluck the string. The bell tone is called a harmonic. These frets include the fifth, seventh, and twelfth.

guitar from the list price. The trick is to get him to do that for you. To make that happen, remember these tips:

- **Keep your salesperson on a need-to-know basis:** If you tell him that you're in love with this guitar and have to have it right now, you've tipped your hand, and your discount will be smaller as a result.
- **Keep it casual:** Mention to your salesperson that you've seen a lot of nice guitars in other stores around town. Also, try out a few other guitars besides the one you've got your eye on, including some that are cheaper (read: smaller commission), so your salesperson will be happy when you "gravitate" toward your beloved selection. And don't appear to be in any hurry to buy a guitar today.
- **Know if the price you're being quoted includes a case:** If so, ask if the case is a hardshell case or a soft gig bag. This is significant because a hardshell case sells for around $100, and a gig bag sells for around $40, on average.
- **Never, ever pay list price for a guitar!** No music store today could stay in business if it sold its instruments for list price when 30 percent discounts are commonplace.

Once you've negotiated your discount there's another move you can make, which is asking your salesperson to throw in some guitar accessories free of charge (or at least at a heavily discounted price). These items might include anything on the Basic Accessories list that follows, including extra strings, picks, and a capo.

Before you plunk down your money, there's one more subject to discuss with your salesperson—the store's return policy. You should have the right to return your instrument for any reason, no questions asked, for at least a week after your purchase date, for a full refund (possibly less the ubiquitous "restocking fee") or an exchange. Just for reference, Guitar Center has a thirty-day return policy, and Sam Ash offers forty-five days. Make sure you clearly understand the return policy that will apply to your purchase.

Basic Accessories

Once you have your guitar, you're going to need a guitar case to protect it. Hardshell cases offer the best protection. Soft gig bags are lighter and have shoulder straps but offer limited protection. In addition to a case, you'll also need a few other important accessories:

- **Electronic tuner:** Before this baby was invented, every guitarist had his own way of tuning his instrument wrong. A must-have! The Korg CA-30 is one excellent tuner that works great for acoustic guitars at a low price.
- **Guitar strap:** If you want to play standing up, you'll need this. Check your instrument for strap buttons on the base and at the neck end of the body; if there's no button for the strap on the neck end, you'll need a strap that ties above the nut on the headstock.
- **Extra strings:** Without them, a broken string is a show-stopper. Make sure you have at least one extra for every string on the guitar.
- **Guitar picks:** Buy them by the dozen, especially if you use the kind that break easily, such as Fender thins. Keep a few in your pocket at all times!
- **Capo:** This device allows you to change the key of your guitar by clamping the strings down at any fret you choose.
- **Slide:** If you want to play slide guitar (which every guitarist should try) you'll need one of these. Slides come in glass

ASK YOUR GUIDE

Can I get past my shyness about price haggling?

▶ Many people have difficulties bringing up the subject of getting a discount with a salesperson. Here's the way I approach the issue: Ask the salesperson to give you the whole price, including tax and case, for the guitar. When he or she gives you the final quote, say "Hmmm, now what can you do for me to get that price a little lower?" Have a price in mind—I often aim for a 15 percent discount. If you know of a store that offers a lower price for the same guitar, make the salesperson aware of that. You might have to use a little bit of pressure, but it's something you'll get used to doing.

(which has the smoothest sound and the longest sustain), smooth chrome-finished metal, and brushed metal (which adds its own little textured sound to the slide).

- **Humidifier:** Changes in humidity affect the wood in an acoustic guitar, sometimes with disastrous results. A humidifier can dramatically reduce the effects of changing humidity on your acoustic guitar.
- **Guitar stand:** Having your guitar sitting out on a guitar stand—say right next to your favorite chair—will boost the time you spend practicing enormously!
- **Maintenance kit:** These kits contain items including guitar polish, special cleaning fluids for the fingerboard and the strings, and polishing cloths for keeping your instrument clean and shiny.

Most music stores offer some instruments in package deals that include items listed above. As long as the guitar in question is the one you want, go with the flow! But don't buy a cheaper instrument or one you like less just because it's part of a package deal.

Get Linked

You can find more information on the subjects we've discussed in this chapter on my **About.com** *site. Check out these helpful links.*

BRANDS OF GUITARS

Links to major guitar companies' Web sites
http://about.com/guitar/brands

GUITAR REVIEWS ARCHIVE

Archive of reviews of instruments by guitarists
http://about.com/guitar/reviewarchive

THE ABOUT.COM GUITAR FORUM

Discussion board for guitarists—check out the Guitars and Equipment section
http://about.com/guitar/forum

Chapter 2

Introduction to Your Instrument

The Adventure Begins

Now that you've selected and acquired your instrument, it's time to learn what to do with it! These guitar lessons are designed for people who own (or have borrowed) a guitar, but don't yet know the first thing about playing it. If the guitar is new to you, this chapter will familiarize you with what the different parts of the instrument are called, how to hold your guitar, how to select and hold a guitar pick, and the correct positions for both of your hands. If you're already familiar with the material being covered in this chapter, feel free to skip ahead in the book.

Among other tools you'll need for this endeavor is patience. If you want to learn to play guitar and if you're willing to practice for fifteen minutes every day (to begin with), you're going to improve—that's a fact. Don't expect to be good right away, because almost nobody is. These are new concepts you're dealing with and it will take a little time for you to understand and master them, but once you get into playing guitar your progress will speed up as the excitement of getting each new chord and riff gives you the energy you need to learn the next one. This is the beginning of a lifelong adventure!

Parts of the Guitar

Acoustic guitars come in many types, shapes, and sizes, but there are certain things they all have in common. Let's look at the different parts of the instrument and what they're called.

At the top of the guitar is the **headstock**, also referred to as the **tuning head**. Attached to the headstock are the **tuners** or **tuning machines**, which you will use to adjust the pitch of each string on your guitar.

At the end of the neck, just below the headstock, is a small piece called the **nut**. This is a little block made out of plastic, bone, composite, or metal that has six small grooves cut into it to guide the strings up to the tuning machines.

The **neck** of the guitar is the long piece between the headstock and the body. The **fingerboard**, or **fretboard**, is usually a separate piece of hard wood that's glued onto the front of the neck. Set into the fingerboard are the **frets**, small rounded strips of metal that rise above the surface of the fingerboard. Also set flush into the fingerboard are **inlays**, which are round dots or other shapes used to mark your position on the neck as you play. There are dots for the same purpose set into the upper edge of the fingerboard.

The neck is an area of the instrument we'll concentrate on a great deal. As you put your fingers on various places on the neck you'll create different notes, melodies, and chords. That makes it worth taking a moment here to look at the two different meanings of the word "frets." The first meaning refers to the strips of metal themselves, while the second refers to the spaces on the neck between one strip of metal and the next. The area of the neck

▶ You'll need only a few things for these guitar lessons. First, and most obviously, a guitar, preferably with 6 strings (12-string guitars are not recommended for beginners). Next, you'll need a guitar pick. Medium-gauge is recommended for beginners (see the discussion about choosing a pick later in this chapter). To practice comfortably, you should have a chair without arms. This will allow you to sit up straight with your back against the back rest and will allow the instrument to rest properly. Finally, you need a music stand, which will place your music, this book, and any other study materials right at eye level.

between the nut and the first strip of metal is called the first fret, and so is the first strip of metal. That's because pressing your finger on the first space holds the string down behind the first strip of metal, creating the intended note. The space between the first and second metal frets is the second fret, and so is the second metal fret. Get it?

The **body** of the acoustic guitar is composed of the **top**, **sides**, and **back**. The top, or **face**, of the instrument lies just below the strings. The **sound hole** is the round hole in the center of the top, from which the sound of the instrument emanates. The sides are the narrow pieces between the front and the back, which is the large surface parallel to the top. Generally the back and sides of the instrument are made out of the same kind of wood, while on the majority of instruments the top is a finer, thinner piece of wood (or laminate in the case of less expensive guitars) because it is the top that most defines the overall sound of the guitar.

Some acoustic guitars have a piece of plastic, called a **pick guard**, glued to the top just below the sound hole. Just as it sounds, this is designed to protect the top of the instrument from damage inflicted by your pick.

The **bridge** is the block of wood glued to the top of the guitar that anchors the strings to the body. The strings pass over the **saddle**, which is a hard, thin piece of plastic, bone, or composite, before their ends are secured into the bridge.

The **strings** of the guitar generate the sound of the instrument when they vibrate. On steel-string guitars the end of the string has a little metal "ball" attached to it. The ball end of the string is pushed down through a hole in the bridge, where it is held in position by a **bridge pin**, which is a plastic pin with a round top and a groove cut into one side to allow for the string. The string then bends over the saddle, runs over the length of the neck, bends over the nut, and is tied onto the peg of the tuning machine. The

ELSEWHERE ON THE WEB

▶ Mark Vassberg, a guitarist in Austin, Texas, has a clear, easy-to-understand image of an acoustic guitar with the parts labeled on his Web site. Just go to www .vassberg.net/acoustic guitar/labeled.shtml. Note that this diagram mentions one other part of the guitar that we haven't discussed, which is the "heel" of the neck—the part of the neck that attaches to the body of the instrument.

ELSEWHERE ON THE WEB

▶ Frets.com is a great guitar site you might want to check out. Among other helpful tips, it has some good advice from a well-respected guitar repair source about where to install a second strap button on your acoustic guitar. Just go to www.frets.com/FRETS Pages/Musician/GenSetup/ StrapButton/strapbutton2 .html.

point at which the string passes over the saddle defines one end of the playable part of the string, while the point at which the string passes over the nut defines the other end of the playable string. Classical nylon strings have no ball on the end, so they tie onto the bridge instead.

At the base of the guitar is a little plastic or metal button called a **strap button**, onto which the guitar strap buttons. Most acoustic guitars don't have a second strap button, so the other end of the strap is meant to tie onto the headstock above the nut. It is possible to mount a second button—which many guitarists want—at the base of the neck (see link at left for more info).

Now that you've learned the parts of the acoustic guitar, take some time to commit them to memory. You'll be referring to them often in conversations with other guitarists and with music store salespeople. Test yourself by pointing to different parts of the guitar at random and saying the name of that part at the same time.

Holding Your Guitar

Okay—it's time to pick up your guitar and learn how to hold it when you play. You'll need an armless chair to sit on. Sit down with your back straight and both feet on the floor in front of you. The small of your back should be supported by the back of the chair.

Note that this sitting-up-straight position is what you should aim for every time you play guitar in a sitting position. Trying to play while lying back on the couch with your instrument resting almost horizontally against your chest, for example, puts your fretting hand in an awkward and uncomfortable position that's not conducive to playing well.

Now pick up your guitar. If you're right-handed, the lower side of the body of the instrument will rest on your right leg (which fits neatly into the curve of the guitar's side), with the neck extending to your left. The back of the guitar will rest against the right side of your chest and upper stomach. The fingerboard of the guitar should be perpendicular to the floor, meaning that the guitar is not leaning forward or backward.

If you're left-handed, everything I just said will be the opposite: Your guitar will rest on your left leg with the neck extending to the right, and the back of the guitar will rest against the left side of your chest and upper stomach. One more thing: You're going to need a **left-handed guitar**, because if you try to play a right-handed guitar in this position the strings will be upside down. I have met one person who could play like this, but he was a freak of nature!

When your guitar is in the correct position, the thickest, lowest-sounding string will be closest to your face, while the thinnest, highest-sounding string will be closest to the floor.

I suppose I should mention, even if this makes your head explode, that proper classical guitar technique dictates that the right-handed guitarist rest his instrument on his left knee instead of his right, with the neck extending to the left. But for this lesson, let's stick to our initial explanation.

Right Hand Position

Place your right arm over the top of the guitar body and rest it with your elbow just over the upper side of the instrument. Your arm should hang naturally over the front of the guitar in this position. Feels good, right?

How to hold your pick. If you're right-handed, your right hand will be your **picking hand**. With your arm in the position described previously, place your picking hand with the palm facing the strings of the guitar, as if you're about to pat the strings. Then close your hand into a very loose fist with the ball of your thumb resting against the side of the first knuckle of your index finger. Where your thumb and index finger are touching is exactly where you'll

ASK YOUR GUIDE

How does an acoustic guitar work?

▶ When a guitar string is plucked it produces vibration. This vibration is transmitted through the bridge into the body of the instrument, causing the inside of the body to resonate, which in turn causes the front and the back of the body to vibrate. Compressed waves of sound are then created inside the body, which are projected out of the soundhole. To learn more about this, check out the Physics of the Acoustic Guitar at http://ffden-2.phys.uaf.edu/211.web.stuff/billington/main.htm.

hold your pick. Now, use your other hand to slide your guitar pick in between the ball of your thumb and the side of the first knuckle of your index finger, with the point facing the strings and sticking out about half an inch. Hold the pick firmly enough that it won't change position while you pick or strum the strings.

To get your pick in the right place relative to your guitar, position your picking hand, with the knuckle of your thumb facing you, over the strings above the sound hole. Your hand should hover over the strings without resting on the strings or on the body of your guitar.

So, how do you use a pick? There are two things you'll be doing with your pick—one is **strumming** all or most of the strings at once to play **chords**, and the other is **picking** individual strings to play **single-note melodies**, which is sometimes called "playing a **solo**" or "playing **lead**." We'll go into each of these techniques in more depth shortly, but for now here's how to try each one:

To strum the strings, brush the end of the pick across all six strings in one smooth downward motion, using a combination of turning your wrist downward and moving your forearm down from the elbow to move the pick through the strings. Try this a few times until all six strings ring out at the same time and have a smooth, strong sound. You can tell you're strumming too hard if you hear the strings buzz against the frets or produce a rattling sound. Once you have these **downstrokes** sounding good, try an **upstroke**: Brush the pick across all six strings with an upward motion of your forearm, remembering to turn your wrist upward at the same time. Try these upstrokes a few times until you can get all six strings to ring out. Last, try alternating your downstrokes and upstrokes until you can make them sound almost the same in volume and **attack**, the term that describes how hard the pick is hitting the strings.

ELSEWHERE ON THE WEB

▶ Take a look at a photo of what correct fretting-hand position looks like. Note how the hand hangs down below the neck of the guitar, and how the ball of the thumb presses into the back of the neck to add pressure to the fretting fingers. Just go to http://gplayer010.tripod .com/images/thumb_a.jpg.

Picking individual strings requires a much smaller motion, which occurs mostly in the wrist, rather than the arm, of your picking hand. So, using your wrist to create the motion, try pushing the tip of your pick "through" the sixth string (the thickest one, closest to you), using a downward stroke until the note sounds and your pick is resting against the top of the fifth string. If the string buzzes or rattles, try striking the string more softly or with less of the surface of the pick. After you've done this a few times, try picking the sixth string from the bottom, using an upward motion of the wrist. Next, try alternating downstrokes and upstrokes on the sixth string, making your wrist motion with the pick as small as possible. Try to make your downstrokes and upstrokes sound as much the same as possible. This process is known as alternate picking. Last, try the same alternate picking exercise on each of the remaining five strings.

Left Hand Position

Now let's concentrate on your fretting hand, which for right-handed people is the left hand.

The thumb of your fretting hand should rest behind the neck of the guitar, while your fingers curl up from beneath the neck to hover above the strings. It's extremely important to keep your fingers curled at the knuckles (except when specifically instructed not to) so that your fingers are positioned to press the strings against the fingerboard with their very tips, as opposed to the pads below the fingertips. This correct hand position will make it much easier for you to play clean-sounding chords when you begin playing in the next lesson.

Choosing a Pick

Guitar picks come in many different shapes, weights, materials, and designs. As far as shapes are concerned, the most common is the

ELSEWHERE ON THE WEB

▶ If you want to look at a sampling of the many guitar picks that are out there, take a look at the Musician's Friend site. You'll see examples of all the types of picks we're discussing. Check out the wide variety of shapes, sizes, weights, grip feature options, materials, and designs that are available. Just go to www.musiciansfriend.com and type "guitar picks" into the search box.

How do I know what kind of pick is right for me?

▶ You can experiment with different shapes, gauges, materials, and designs until you find the picks you like the best. Go to the music store and select a couple of each type that appeals to you. Be sure to get some thin, medium, and heavy gauges. Also, try some cel- luloid picks and some nylon picks, as well as some picks with special grip features. You'll have favorites in no time. In the meantime, I highly recommend that you start with medium-gauge picks, which are neither too flimsy nor too hard.

Fender "351" shape, a rounded oblong triangle that is now offered by most pick manufacturers. There are also triangle shapes and teardrop shapes with various degrees of pointy-ness or roundness. And then there are a few "out there" shapes, each of which seems to come with a theory about why that shape is what the world has been missing up until now.

Picks basically come in thin, medium, and thick gauges, or weights. Thin picks are very flexible and easy to sweep across the strings, so they're generally considered to be better for strumming chords, while heavy picks are often preferred for playing single-note melodies because it's easier to precisely control the point of a heavier pick. Medium-gauge picks offer a compromise between these two ideas, giving you the flexibility to strum as well as some degree of point control.

There are two things that seem to go wrong with picks repeat-edly when you're playing. These are (A) they break, and (B) they fly out of your hand, possibly getting lost. Of course Murphy's Law dictates that these things usually happen right in the middle of a song. The good news is that pick manufacturers have solutions for both problems, which is where the different materials and designs come into play.

Picks that break are usually made of celluloid, which is a nice, flex-ible material that also has a tendency to tear. To avoid this problem you can select picks made of nylon, which will never tear, even in their thinnest gauges. One example of a good nylon pick is the Jim Dunlop USA Nylon series, which come in thin, medium, and heavy gauges.

Picks that easily fly out of your hand are also usually made of celluloid, which can be very slippery in your hand—especially if you're sweating. To avoid this problem you can select picks that have grip features built in, including a hole through the pick where your fingers grip it, a hole with cork rings around it on both sides of the pick, and various textured, indented, or rubberized grips.

Get Linked

*You can find more information on the subjects we've discussed in this chapter on my **About.com** site. Check out these helpful links.*

PARTS OF THE GUITAR

Photos of an acoustic guitar with the parts labeled and a close-up of the guitar neck

↗ http://about.com/guitar/guitarparts

HOW TO HOLD YOUR PICK

Photo of the correct way to hold your pick

↗ http://about.com/guitar/holdpick

About.

Chapter 3

Guitar Basics

Names of the Strings

Congratulations! You've made it to the chapter where you'll begin to play the guitar. This is where the fun starts. By the time we get through this chapter you'll be able to play whole songs as well as some lead guitar. There's just a little more technical talk we need to cover before we start playing.

The first thing another guitar player will say to you when you get together to play is, "give me an E," referring to an open string on your guitar. You'll want to speak the language too, and this is a good place to start.

Every fret on every string of the guitar produces a note, and every note has a name, which is represented by a letter. The names of each of the notes on your instrument are important; you'll need to know where to find them in order to read music or to communicate with other musicians. We'll look at the notes on every string as we go along, but for now let's start with the names of the six open strings on the guitar.

Figure 3–1   Names of the
open strings

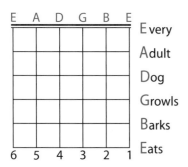

Figure 3–1 illustrates the names of the open strings on the guitar. Going from the sixth string (thickest) to the first string (thinnest), the strings are named E, A, D, G, B, and E.

The sixth string and the first string are the same note, two octaves apart.

Because you're going to need to know the names of your strings for so many reasons, take the time to learn them now. To help you memorize them, try this little phrase: "**E**very **A**dult **D**og **G**rowls, **B**arks, and **E**ats."

Try playing each of the strings in order while saying the names out loud as an exercise. Then test yourself by pointing to a string at random and saying the name of that string as quickly as possible. When you can name them all, in any random order, in less than ten seconds, you've passed the test!

Tuning Your Guitar

Before you play your guitar you'll have to get it in tune. Most beginners are a little confused by this process, but it becomes second nature pretty fast, and it's essential to sounding good on guitar.

Use a reference pitch. If you aren't using a chromatic tuner you'll need a reference pitch from another source. This could come from another guitar or a piano, in which case an E would be a good pitch to tune to since you can tune your bottom and top strings right off. Or it could come from a **tuning fork**, which is a piece of metal shaped like a wishbone—you strike the double end against your hand to make it vibrate, and then touch the single end against the body of your guitar or against your ear to hear the note.

To find an E on the piano use the black keys as a reference. They appear in groups of three and two, and E is the white key just to the right of the group of two black keys. Note that the E you play on the piano may not be in the same octave as the low E string on your guitar. If the E you play on the piano sounds much higher or lower than your low E string, try playing the different Es on the piano until you find the one closest to your open sixth string.

If you use a tuning fork, the note it produces will probably be an A (also marked 440 on the fork, which is the number of **cycles per second** of that note), so you would use it to tune your fifth string, and then tune the rest of your guitar around that string.

If you're on a desert island without your tuning fork, or don't have access to a reference pitch for any other reason, you can still tune your guitar to itself (meaning that the strings will be in correct tune relative to each other even if their pitches aren't exactly right) and it will sound fine on its own. But if you want to play with other instruments you'll need to be tuned to **real pitch**.

Tune the other strings of the guitar. Assuming you've got your sixth string in tune, let's move on to learning how to tune the rest of the strings. You can see a diagram of how to tune the other strings relative to a tuned sixth string on my About.com site: http://about.com/guitar/howtotune.

As you can see from the diagram, if you play the fifth fret of your sixth (E) string, the resulting note will be an A, which is the pitch your fifth string is supposed to be. If you play the fifth fret of your fifth (A) string, the resulting note will be D, which is the pitch your fourth string is supposed to be. The only time this pattern changes is when you tune the second (B) string to the third (G) string—in that case you play the fourth fret of the G string to hear the B you need to tune the second string. Give it a try!

Here are some steps to follow to tune your guitar:

1. Make sure your sixth string is in tune.
2. Play the sixth string, fifth fret (A), then tune your open fifth string (A) until they sound the same.

3. Play the fifth string, fifth fret (D), then tune your open fourth string (D) until they sound the same.

4. Play the fourth string, fifth fret (G), then tune your open third string (G) until they sound the same.

5. Play the third string, **fourth** fret (B), then tune your open second string (B) until they sound the same.

6. Play the second string, fifth fret (E), then tune your open first string (E) until they sound the same. Then double-check your first string against your sixth string—they should be the same.

Start training your ear. If you can tell when two notes sound different from each other, but are having a hard time telling which is higher and which is lower, the following is an exercise that can help.

Pick two notes that are fairly close together on your guitar. Play the first note and listen to it and then, while the note is still ringing, try humming that note. Continue to play the first note until you've managed to match the pitch with your voice. Then play the second note, listen to it, and try to hum that note while it's still ringing. When you've matched the pitch of the second note with your voice, try alternating the two notes, picking and humming the first note and then the second, back and forth. Last, try just humming the first note and, without stopping, move to the second note. Did your voice go up or down when you moved to the second note? If it went down, the second note is lower. If it went up, the second note is higher.

Next time you try this exercise, use two notes that are even closer together. Soon you'll be able to recognize the difference in pitches without having to hum them, and you'll know which pitch is higher or lower. Remember to tune your guitar before you play it—every time! It will make your playing sound a whole lot better, and the practice in tuning will quickly make you good at this critical task.

When you first start playing you probably won't be able to tell whether your instrument is in tune or not. There's a great resource on my About.com site where you can listen to an MP3 file of a fully tuned guitar on your computer. Each string is played twice, so you can tune your guitar against it as you listen. Just go to http://about .com/guitar/audiotuning.

Introduction to Scales

There are two skills on guitar that will play a big part in your overall musicianship. One is playing **scales**, which will drive your ability to play single-note melodies—also known as **lead guitar**. The other is playing chords, which will drive your ability to play songs, or **rhythm guitar**.

To learn scales and chords you'll need to understand the fingering notation that appears on most chord and some scale diagrams. On these diagrams you'll see the numbers 1, 2, 3, and 4, which correspond to the four fingers on your fretting hand, the one that plays notes on the neck of your guitar. Take a look at your fretting hand right now, with the palm facing up: Your index finger is 1, your middle finger is 2, your ring finger is 3, and your pinky is 4. In some chords your thumb will even get into the act, so it has an identifier too, which is the letter *T*.

We'll begin with scales. In order to become skillful on the guitar, you'll need to strengthen the muscles in your hands, learn to stretch your fingers, and build finger dexterity. Scales are a good way to do all of these things.

Let's learn a scale now. We'll begin with a **chromatic scale**, which uses all twelve notes in the octave. If you know the piece "Flight of the Bumblebee" you'll remember what a chromatic scale sounds like.

How often should I tune my guitar, and how long should it take me?

▶ You should tune your guitar every single time you pick it up. Guitars (particularly cheaper ones) tend to go out of tune quickly. Make sure it's in tune when you begin to play it, and check the tuning frequently while you're practicing, as the act of playing the guitar can cause it to go out of tune. At first, it may take you five minutes or more to get your instrument in tune, but the more familiar you are with tuning, the more quickly you'll be able to do it. Many guitarists can get their instrument roughly in tune in about 30 seconds.

Figure 3-2 might look confusing at first, but don't worry—it's one of the most common methods of illustrating notes on the guitar, and it's quite easy to understand. It's simply a picture that represents the neck of the guitar when you look at it head-on.

Figure 3-2   The neck of the guitar

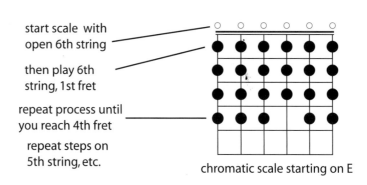

start scale with
open 6th string

then play 6th
string, 1st fret

repeat process until
you reach 4th fret

repeat steps on
5th string, etc.

chromatic scale starting on E

The first vertical line on the left of the **diagram** is the sixth string, the vertical line to the right of that is the fifth string, and so on.

The first horizontal line on the top of the diagram represents the nut at the end of the neck, the second horizontal line down is the first metal fret, the third horizontal line down is the second metal fret, and so on. And the spaces between the horizontal lines represent the frets on the fingerboard where your fingers are placed (between the metal frets) to create the notes.

The little *O* above the strings in the diagram indicates that you're supposed to play the open string (which is playing the string with no fingers pressed on it) that the *O* is positioned above.

Finally, the black dots indicate the notes that should be played.

To play a scale on guitar you generally begin with the notes on the sixth string, from lowest to highest, then move to the notes on the fifth string, and so on until you've played the highest note on the first string. This is called an **ascending scale**. Once you've got that down, try playing the same scale in reverse order starting with the highest dot on the first string and going backward until you reach the open note on the sixth string. This is called a **descending scale**.

To play the chromatic scale diagrammed in **Figure 3–2**, start by using your pick to play the open sixth string. Next, place the first finger of your fretting hand (remembering to curl the finger) on the first fret of the sixth string (where the first black dot is). Be sure to apply enough downward pressure to the string so that you're producing a clear note, and strike the string with your pick. Now, place your second finger on the second fret of the guitar where the second black dot is (you can take your first finger off of the first fret), and again strike the sixth string with the pick. Now, repeat the same process on the third fret, using your third finger. Finally, play the fourth fret, using your fourth finger. There! You've played all the notes on the sixth string.

Now, move to the fifth string. Start by playing the open string, and then play frets one, two, three, and four. Repeat this process for each string. Note that on the third string you play only up to the third fret. When you've played all the way up to the first string, fourth fret, you've completed the ascending chromatic scale. You can listen to an MP3 file of the chromatic scale on my About.com site: http://about.com/guitar/audiochromatic.

Here are some tips to help you with your scales:

- Use alternate picking (going back and forth between down-strokes and upstrokes) with this exercise. If this is overwhelming, try using only downstrokes with your pick, but go back to alternate picking once you've gotten used to the scale.
- Once you've finished the ascending scale, try playing the scale backward by starting at the first string, fourth fret, and playing all notes in exactly the reverse order.

▶ Here's a tip to help you with your scales: When playing a note, place your finger at the "top of fret" (the area of the fingerboard between the metal frets that's farthest away from the headstock). This will produce a clearer sound.

Figure 3–3   G major chord

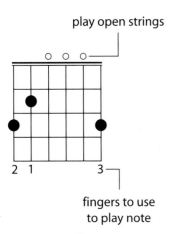

play open strings

2   1   3

fingers to use
to play note

Introduction to Chords

Although practicing the previous chromatic scale is guaranteed to limber up your fingers, it's not what you'd call a whole lot of fun. I know you're itching to start playing chords on the guitar, so let's get going!

Playing a chord involves using your pick to strike two or more notes simultaneously. We'll start with three of the most common and easy-to-play chords on the guitar.

Figure 3–3 illustrates the first chord we're going to learn, a G major chord, which is often referred to simply as a G chord.

You'll notice that the chord diagram has a thick horizontal line on the top—this represents the nut of your guitar. Just as on scale diagrams, the vertical lines on chord diagrams represent the six strings on your guitar; the horizontal lines below the nut represent the metal frets; and the dots show you where your fingers go. The Os above the nut tell you to include those open strings as part of the chord, and the numbers below the dots tell you which finger to use for each note.

To play the G major chord, place your second finger on the third fret of the sixth string. Now put your first finger on the second fret of the fifth string. Finally, place your third finger on the third fret of the first string. Make sure all of your fingers are curled so that you're pressing the strings down with the very tips of your fingers, and that none of your fingers are touching any strings they're not supposed to. Now use your pick to strike all six strings in one fluid motion. The notes should ring all at once, not one at a time (remember your strumming from Chapter 2). There it is—your first chord!

Now test yourself to make sure that each note in your G chord is ringing out clearly. To do this, start with the sixth string and play each string one at a time, listening to make sure that each note is clear and strong. When you play the notes of a chord one at a time it's known as an arpeggio. If any of the notes sound "dead" or muffled, it's either because you're not pressing the string down against the fingerboard hard enough, or because one of your other fingers is touching the string when it shouldn't be.

The next chord we'll learn is the C major chord, also known as a C chord. You'll notice a new notation on **Figure 3–4**, which is the X above the sixth string. This means that you are not to play this string as part of the chord.

To play the C major chord, place your third finger on the third fret of the fifth string. Then put your second finger on the second fret of the fourth string. Finally, put your first finger on the first fret of the second string.

Remember—the X above the sixth string is telling you NOT to play the low E string as part of the C major chord. So when you play this chord, make sure you only strum the bottom five strings.

Now test this chord the same way you tested your G major chord: Play each of the five notes one at a time to make sure that each note is ringing out clearly.

The last chord we'll learn in this lesson is the D major chord, also called a D chord (**Figure 3–5**). To play the D major chord, place your first finger on the second fret of the third string. Then put your third finger on the third fret of the second string. Last, place your second finger on the second fret of the first string.

Note that the Xs above the sixth and fifth strings are telling you NOT to play those two strings as part of your D major chord. But the O above the fourth string tells you that you do include the fourth string, played open. So when you play this chord, make sure you only strum the bottom four strings. Now test this chord to make sure that each note is ringing out clearly.

Take the time to really learn these three chords. You'll be using them for the rest of your guitar-playing career. Make sure you can play each one without having to look at the diagrams. By the time you're done practicing you should know the name of each chord, where each finger goes to play it, and which strings you strum.

Figure 3–4   C major chord

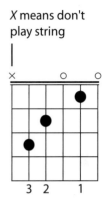

X means don't play string

3 2   1

Figure 3–5   D major chord

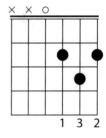

1 3 2

Songs You Can Play Now

Now you know three chords—G major, C major, and D major. Here's some good news: There are a lot of songs that you can play using just these three chords! We'll look at three of them below.

At first, switching from one chord to another will take you too long to play any songs straight through without stopping. Don't give up! The more you practice, the faster and easier switching chords will become. In the next chapter we'll go more in-depth about how to switch chords quickly, as well as learn a couple of strumming patterns, so when you come back to these songs you'll be able to play them much better.

▶ ▶ ▶
Here are the links to the songs you can play already. The first two come from my About.com site, and the third comes from Chordie.com, which is an excellent resource for song lyrics and chords.

- ○ "Leaving on a Jet Plane," *words and music by John Denver*
  www.geocities.com/etheltheaardvark/jetplane.txt

- ○ "The Gambler," *words and music by Kenny Rogers*
  www.geocities.com/etheltheaardvark/gambler.txt

- ○ "La Bamba," *the Los Lobos version*
  www.chordie.com/chord.pere/www.ultimate-guitar.com/print
  .php?what=tab&id=9407&1944-06-06=always&tuning=
  EADGBE&transpose=-5

When you start with "Leaving on a Jet Plane," note that this particular chord notation includes slashes above the lyrics. In this instance, both the chord symbols and the slashes represent one beat, as a way to tell you when to switch chords and how long to hold them. Each **measure**, or **bar**, of this song is four beats long, and each line of the lyrics is two measures long. So the first line, "All my bags are packed, I'm ready to go" would be counted 1-2-3-4 1-2-3-4. The G chord over the word "bags" is the 1, and the three slashes after it tell you to keep strumming that chord for three more beats, the 2-3-4. The C over "ready" is the 1 of the second measure, and the three slashes after that tell you to keep strumming that chord for three more beats, the 2-3-4. Why are there two words in the first line before the G comes in? Because the lyrics actually begin on the 4-count of the previous measure in this song.

If you want to improve on guitar, practice is essential. Plan to spend at least fifteen minutes each day practicing all the things we've covered in this chapter. Developing a daily routine is a good idea. Try to figure out the best time during your day to play guitar, and make that your regular "practice time." Learning to relax and loosen up while playing guitar will help immeasurably, so be sure to have fun while you practice! At first your fingers will get sore fairly quickly, but by playing daily they'll toughen up, and in a short amount of time they'll stop hurting when you play.

I recommend that, as a new guitarist, you spend at least one week learning the exercises and songs in this chapter before moving on. The following list should give you an idea of how to spend your daily practice time:

1. Get your guitar in tune.
2. Make sure you're sitting, holding the guitar, and using your pick properly. You'll have to correct your natural bad habits at first, until proper form becomes second nature.
3. Play the ascending chromatic scale several times. Then try playing it backward.
4. Play each of the three chords you've learned, checking to be sure each note is ringing clearly. If any are not, find out why, and correct the problem.
5. Try moving from one chord to another. Before switching chords, mentally picture exactly where each finger is going to move in order to play the next chord. Only then should you switch chords. This is the key to switching chords quickly.

WHAT'S HOT

▶ Having trouble making your chords ring out clearly? The most common problem in this situation is that you're trying to fret the notes in the chord with the pads of your fingers, when you should be using the very tips. To learn more, check out the feature on my site about overcoming dead and muffled strings. You'll learn the proper way to grip the neck of your guitar, as well as the most common mistakes and how to avoid them. Just visit http://about.com/guitar/playingchords.

6. Try playing some or all of the songs listed in this chapter. At first, try to think of the songs as just a way to practice playing chords.

If you're not able to do all these things right off the bat, don't get discouraged. This is hard stuff at first, and you'll probably have moments when you feel like you can't do it. But I'm here to tell you that you certainly can! Everyone starts as a beginner, and everyone struggles, so just put in your fifteen minutes and then don't worry about it until the next time you play. This is supposed to be fun!

Get Linked

*You can find more information about the subjects we've discussed in this chapter on my **About.com** site. Check out these helpful links.*

HISTORY OF THE GUITAR

Here's where you can learn more about the history of the guitar.

↗ http://about.com/guitar/history

Chapter 4

Focus on Chords

Introduction to Minor Chords

In Chapter 3 you learned your first three chords: G major, C major, and D major. What do those three chords have in common? They're all **major chords**. In this chapter we'll explore another type of chord—the **minor chord**.

The terms "major" and "minor" are used to describe the sound of the chord. In very basic terms, a major chord sounds happy, while a minor chord sounds sad. Most songs contain a combination of both major and minor chords.

Let's start with an E minor chord, which is an easy chord that requires only two fingers of your fretting hand to play (**Figure 4–1**). Start by placing your second finger on the second fret of the fifth string. Then place your third finger on the second fret of the fourth string. Strum all six strings and there you have it—an E minor chord!

Remember to test yourself to make sure that each note in your chord is ringing out clearly. To do this, start with the sixth string and play each string, one at a time, listening to make sure that each

Figure 4–1   E minor chord

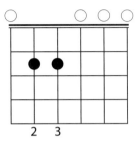

Figure 4–2   A minor chord

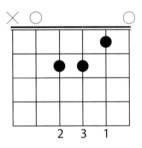

Figure 4–3   D minor chord

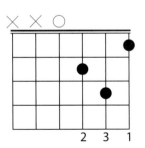

note is clear and strong. If any of the notes sound "dead" or muffled, it's either because you're not pressing the string down against the fingerboard hard enough, or because one of your other fingers is touching the string when it shouldn't be. Figure out what the problem is and adjust your fingering until the problem goes away.

Now let's try an A minor chord (**Figure 4–2**). Start by placing your second finger on the second fret of the fourth string. Then place your third finger on the second fret of the third string. Last, place your first finger on the first fret of the second string. You'll note that the A minor chord diagram has an X over the sixth string, which means you don't play that string as part of this chord. Strum the bottom five strings (being careful to avoid the sixth), and you're playing an A minor chord. Now check each string to make sure all the individual notes are ringing clearly.

The last minor chord we'll play now is a D minor chord (**Figure 4–3**). Start by placing your first finger on the first fret of the first string. Then put your second finger on the second fret of the third string. Finally, place your third finger on the third fret of the second string. Note that there are Xs over both the sixth and the fifth string in the D minor chord diagram, so you strum only the bottom four strings to play this chord. Give it a try. Then check each of the four strings to make sure the individual notes are ringing clearly.

In Chapter 3 you learned to play a D major chord, so this is a good opportunity to study the difference between a major and a minor chord. In case you don't remember it, see the D major chord (**Figure 4–4**). Play the D major chord four times in a row, and then play the D minor chord four times. Play this alternating pattern a few times as your ear gets used to the two chord sounds.

If you'd like to hear the difference between a major chord and a minor chord in the same key, check out this sound file on my About.com site. You'll hear A major, A minor, A major, and A minor again. You'll note that the major chord has a bright, optimistic ring to it, while the minor chord has a darker, sadder sound. Listen closely; it goes by pretty quickly. Just go to http://about.com/guitar/audioamajmin.

More Major Chords

There are three more major chords we should look at now. Once you've learned these you'll know all of what are considered to be the basic open chords, which means you'll be able to play a lot of songs!

The E major chord is the bedrock chord of the guitar (**Figure 4–5**). It has an especially powerful sound when played in open position because both the sixth string and the first string are ringing out open E notes, in addition to the E note that's being played on the fourth string. The majority of blues songs are in the key of E, and so are the majority of rock songs, no doubt because the guitar has been the driving instrument behind both of these genres. Translation: You're going to love this chord!

Start by placing your second finger on the second fret of the fifth string. Then place your third finger on the second fret of the fourth string. Last, place your first finger on the first fret of the third string. Note that there are Os over the sixth, second, and first strings on the E major chord diagram, so you'll strum all six strings. Now hit that E major chord with one strong downstroke and feel the power! As always, check each string individually, starting with the sixth string, to make sure the notes are ringing clearly.

The A major chord presents a new fingering challenge: You've got to fit three of your fingers on the second fret right next to each other, and that can feel a little crowded at first (**Figure 4–6**). Start by placing your first finger on the second fret of the fourth string. Then put your second finger on the second fret on the third string. Finally, place your third finger on the second fret of the second string. Note that the A major chord diagram has an X over the sixth string. Strum just the bottom five strings, and you'll have your A major chord.

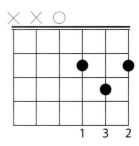

Figure 4–4   D major chord

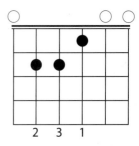

Figure 4–5   E major chord

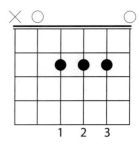

Figure 4–6   A major chord

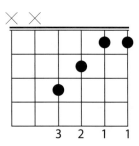

Figure 4–7 F major chord

Another way to play the A major chord is to use your second, third, and fourth fingers on the second fret of the D, G, and B strings. Yet another way is to flatten the end of one finger across all three of those strings. Try all three fingerings, because they'll all be useful to you at various points in your playing.

I saved the F major chord for last because it's a toughie. As the saying goes, "It's not called an F-chord for nothing!" This chord presents another new fingering challenge, which is using your first finger to press down two strings at once (**Figure 4–7**). Note the *1*s below both the second string and the first string in the fingering notation.

To play this chord, place your first finger across the first frets of both the first and second strings. Now, slightly roll the finger back (toward the headstock of the guitar). This will make placing your second and third fingers feel more natural. Then place your second finger on the second fret of the third string. Finally, place your third finger on the third fret of the fourth string. Note that there are Xs above the sixth and fifth string on the F major chord diagram, so you'll strum only the bottom four strings. Strum them now, and let's see what you've got. Chances are, if you're like most new guitarists, few if any of the notes are ringing clearly as you strum this new chord. The good news? Now that you've tried it, you're entitled to use the F-chord joke with firsthand experience!

To master this bad boy, make sure that:

- Your first finger is covering both the second and first string
- You've rolled your first fingertip back slightly toward the headstock
- You're pressing your first finger down hard enough to get clear notes on both strings
- Your second and third fingers are curled so that you're pressing the strings down with the very tips of those fingers
- Each note is ringing clearly

The F major chord can be frustrating (hey—another F word) at first, but keep it on your daily practice list and you'll have it sounding great within weeks.

Moving Between Chords

Congratulations! You've learned all nine of the basic open chords on guitar. The next step is to memorize them. To help with that process, here are all the chords in one place (**Figure 4–8**).

Figure 4–8 The nine basic chord diagrams

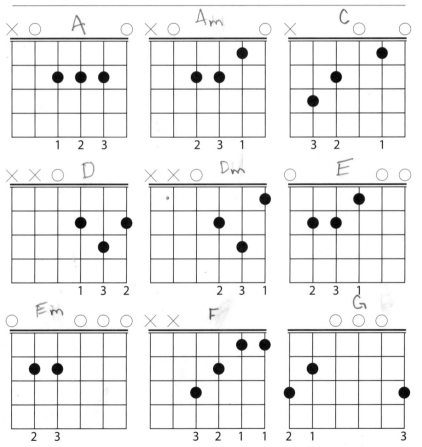

What makes major chords sound happy and minor chords sound sad?

▶ They sound different because a major chord has a major third in its structure, while a minor chord has a minor third in its structure. "Major third" and "minor third" both describe intervals, which means the space between two notes. You can hear the major third in a D major chord by playing your open fourth string and then playing the note on the fourth fret of the fourth string. Now listen to the minor third by playing your open fourth string and then playing the note on the third fret of the fourth string.

WHAT'S HOT

▶ The key to changing chords quickly is to think of the change as one fluid motion in which all of your fingers move at the same time from the old position to the new position, rather than thinking about moving each finger individually. For more information about changing chords quickly, read this article on my About.com site. It will take you through the process one more time. Just go to http://about.com/ guitar/switchingchords.

Getting these chords memorized is just the first step. In order for them to be useful, you'll have to learn to move from chord to chord quickly.

The main reason most beginners have trouble switching chords quickly is because they think of the process as a series of actions, where one finger moves to one fret, and then the next finger moves to another fret, and so on. Take a look at your fingers as you do a chord change. Do they come way off the fingerboard and hover in midair as you try to decide where each finger should go? This creates a lot of wasted motion in your fretting hand and can really slow you down.

To make a quick, clean chord change, all of your fingers have to leave the fingerboard at the same time and land in the new chord position at the same time. The way to make this happen is to play the first chord and then, before you switch to the second chord, visualize your fingers playing the new chord shape. Picture in your mind exactly which fingers will need to go where. When the mental image is clear, make the chord change in one fluid motion. All of your fingers should move into the new chord position at the same time.

As you practice these chords, make it a point to switch from each one to all eight of the others. Watch for any unnecessary movements your fingers make and eliminate them. It's going to take some patience, but soon your chord changes will be quick and confident.

Basic Strumming

One of the primary ways a guitarist can make a song sound good is by adding an interesting strum to the music. A guitarist with a good grasp of strumming can bring a two-chord song to life. In Chapter 2 we looked at the most basic fundamentals of strumming: the downstroke and the upstroke. Now you'll learn how to combine those downstrokes and upstrokes into a couple of basic strumming patterns. Let's look at the first one now.

This pattern is one bar long (**Figure 4–9**). The bar has four counts (1-2-3-4) and eight strums. The arrows along the bottom indicate the direction of the strums—a downward arrow tells you to strum a downstroke, while an upward arrow tells you to strum an upstroke.

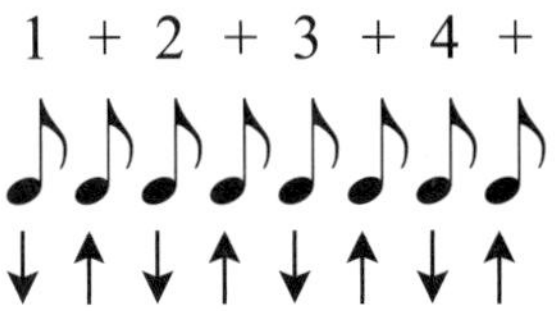

The pattern starts with a downstroke and ends with an upstroke, creating a motion where your strumming arm is swinging down and up continuously. If you play the pattern twice in a row, or any number of times in a row, the down-and-up pattern continues without interruption.

Pick up your guitar and pick and let's give it a try. First establish the rhythm in your head by counting out loud: "1 and 2 and 3 and 4 and 1 and 2 and 3 and 4 and . . ." over and over at a comfortable speed. Place the fingers of your fretting hand lightly on top of all six strings to dampen their sound. Now start strumming your pick down and up across all six strings in a regular rhythm, keeping the same time as your count. Your downstrokes will be on the numbers that you speak, while your upstrokes will be on the *and*s. Try to make the downstrokes and upstrokes sound as much the same as possible, while also keeping the time between the strums exactly the same.

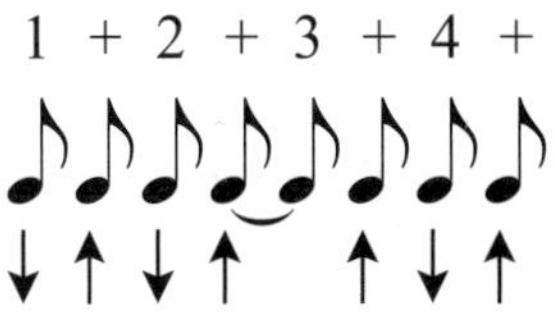

If you're having any problems playing the "1 and 2 and 3 and 4 and" strumming pattern or keeping it steady, you can listen to an MP3 file of it on my About.com site: http://about.com/guitar/audio strum1. The sample is long enough to play along with, too.

Once you have the strum feeling good, use your fretting hand to form a G major chord, and use the same strumming pattern to play the chord.

http://about.com/guitar/audio strum1

Figure 4–9   Strumming pattern #1

Figure 4–10   Strumming pattern #2

How can I make my strumming feel more natural?

▶ To begin with, don't strum too hard or too softly. Strumming too hard can make the strings rattle and buzz, while strumming too softly produces a "wimpy" sound. Your pick should be brushing across the strings with a firm, even stroke. To get that natural feel, think of your elbow as being the top of a pendulum—your arm should swing up and down from it in a steady motion. That said, the bulk of your strumming motion should come from the rotation of your wrist, not from your forearm. Rotate your wrist downward on the downstrokes and upward on the upstrokes.

Now let's try a more challenging variation on this basic strumming pattern (**Figure 4–10**). By simply removing one strum from the previous pattern, you'll be playing one of the most widely used and versatile strumming patterns in pop, country, and rock music!

You can see that the fifth strum of the previous pattern is the one we're dropping out. You might think that the best way to drop that strum is to stop the up-and-down motion of your strumming arm, but that's exactly what you *don't* want to do. Instead, keep the same up-and-down strumming motion going as you did before, playing to your "1 and 2 and 3 and 4 and . . ." count—but when you get to the 3, instead of strumming the downstroke, lift your pick away from the strings and "miss" them with your downstroke. Then lower the pick again so that you're there with the upstroke on the next *and*.

Just to be clear: In this second pattern the up-and-down motion of your strumming arm should not change at all from the first pattern. Deliberately missing the strings with the pick on the third beat of the pattern is the only factor that has changed.

If you're having any problems playing this second strumming pattern or keeping it steady, there's an MP3 file of this one, too, on my About.com site. The sample is long enough to play along with. Just go to http://about.com/guitar/audiostrum2.

It is important that you learn to play this strumming pattern accurately—don't settle for just getting most of the up-and-down strums in the right order. If this strum isn't perfect, it will be virtually impossible for you to learn any harder strums. You should be able to play the pattern many times in a row without having to stop because of an incorrect strum.

Once you can do this, try strumming the pattern at faster speeds.

Songs You Can Play Now

The addition of three minor chords and three new major chords gives you a total of nine chords to learn songs with. Knowing just these nine chords will provide you with the opportunity to play literally hundreds of country, blues, rock, and pop songs.

○ "House of the Rising Sun," *traditional*
www.chordie.com/chord.pere/www.pjandphil.utvinternet.com/
FOLK/RISINGSN.TXT

○ "Mr. Tambourine Man," *Bob Dylan*
http://strongmanthuey.tripod.com/dylan%5Fmrtambourineman.txt

○ "Brown Eyed Girl," *Van Morrison*
http://strongmanthuey.tripod.com/morrison%5Fbrowneyedgirl.txt

I recommend that you practice for at least fifteen minutes each day. If you play guitar every day, even for this small amount of time, you'll quickly get comfortable with the instrument, and you'll be amazed at how fast you progress!

Here's how you should spend your daily practice time:

1. Make sure your guitar is in tune.
2. Go over the chromatic scale and the three major chords from Chapter 3.
3. Review the names of the open strings to be sure you've got them memorized.
4. Spend a good five minutes working on the two strumming patterns. Try the strumming patterns with different chords, playing the strumming patterns with one chord, then switching chords, and playing the pattern again.

◄◄◄
Here are three songs you can try.

5. Play the three minor chords and the three new major chords from this chapter. Say the name of each chord as you play it, to help with memorization. Practice switching from whichever chord you're playing to the eight other ones.

6. Try playing some or all of the songs listed in this chapter. Also, go back and try the songs from Chapter 3. Try to think of the songs as only a way to practice playing chords.

If you find it impossible to fit in practicing all of these things in one sitting, try breaking up the items, and playing them over several days. Don't ignore any of the items on the list, even if they're not a ton of fun to practice. You'll thank me later! As I advised in the last chapter, don't get discouraged. If you can't seem to get something right even after a lot of effort, just shrug your shoulders and leave it for tomorrow.

Get Linked

You can find more information about the subjects we've discussed in this chapter on my **About.com** *site. Check out these helpful links.*

CHORD LIBRARY

Look up any chord you want anytime in the Chord Library.

 http://about.com/guitar/chordlibrary

BLANK SHEET MUSIC

You can print out blank tab paper (for **guitar tablature**, a special notation system you'll learn about in Chapter 7), chord diagrams, or staff paper from this resource.

http://about.com/guitar/blanksheets

Chapter 5

Meet the Blues

Introduction to the Blues Scale

The power of the blues is that it can transform the misery and suffering that inspires it into beautiful music that, ironically, has the ability to heal and make people feel better.

The blues is an American form of folk music with roots in African and European musical culture. Ever since the birth of the blues in the late 1800s in the Mississippi Delta, the guitar has been the primary instrument to drive its development.

When musicians who have never played together before search for common ground, the most frequent call is for a **12-bar blues**, a progression that is so elemental that most musicians know it. If a 50-year-old man and a 14-year-old teenager are trying to play guitar together, chances are they're not going to know many of the same songs—but they will both know how to play a simple blues.

We'll begin with the **blues scale**, which will open up a new universe of ability on guitar to you. That's because the blues scale is a **movable scale**—it uses **closed left-hand fingering**, which means that no open or unfretted strings are used. The beauty of this is that, once you learn the fingering pattern, you'll be able to play this scale in any key you choose, anywhere on the neck. We'll learn the scale on the fifth fret (**Figure 5–1**). Once you're familiar with it, try playing it on the tenth fret, the first fret, and everywhere else.

Figure 5–1   The blues scale

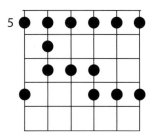

Remember how we identified the fingers on your fretting hand when you learned the chromatic scale? As a refresher, your index finger is 1, your middle finger is 2, your ring finger is 3, and your pinky is 4.

The blues scale is fingered like this: You're starting on the fifth fret, so all notes on the fifth fret will be played by the first finger. All the notes on the sixth fret will be played by the second finger. All notes on the seventh fret will be played by the third finger. Finally, all notes on the eighth fret will be played by the fourth finger.

Place your first finger on the fifth fret of the sixth string, and play that note. Then put your fourth finger on the eighth fret of the sixth string, and again play that note. Now move to the fifth string and play those three notes, and continue to follow the pattern on all the strings until you've reached the eighth fret on the first string. Take your time and learn this scale well—it's one that you will use a lot!

You can listen to a sound file of this blues scale on my About. com site: http://about.com/guitar/audiobluesscale. It's played slowly enough that you should be able to play along.

Things to remember:

- Use alternate picking throughout. Try starting the scale with a downstroke. The next time, try starting the scale with an upstroke.
- Once you've finished the scale, try playing the scale backward by starting at the first string, eighth fret, and playing all notes in exactly the reverse order.
- The key here is accuracy, not speed! Take your time. Try playing the scale very slowly, making sure that each note is ringing clearly.

The blues scale is really just a **pentatonic scale** with a couple of extra **passing notes** (notes that aren't in the scale but ease the passage between one scale note and the next) added. The pentatonic scale is used extensively in playing blues and rock, so you need to be familiar with it.

Most scales have seven notes in them before they reach the next octave. The pentatonic scale is different—it has only five notes between octaves. If you played just the black keys on a piano you would have a pentatonic scale. You might associate the sound with music of the Far East, but when played over a blues chord progression, the pentatonic scale fits right in!

There are two versions of the pentatonic scale, the major and the minor. A pentatonic scale is major if the first interval (the space

TOOLS YOU NEED

▶ A metronome is a simple gadget that emits a steady click at a speed that you can set and vary. Sounds boring, right? Well, they're great for making sure that you keep in time when practicing your scales. These little devices will improve your musicianship incredibly by letting you know right away if you're speeding up or slowing down as you play. Metronomes come in the traditional mechanical version with the arm that swings back and forth, and in electronic versions. They can be found for as little as $20.

between the first and second notes of the scale) is a **major second**, also known as a **whole step**. If the first note of the scale is on the fifth fret, a whole step above that would be the seventh fret.

A pentatonic scale is minor if the first interval is a **minor third**. If the first note of the scale is on the fifth fret, a minor third above that would be the eighth fret. We'll be starting with the minor pentatonic scale (**Figure 5–2**), which can be played over both major and minor blues progressions.

Figure 5–2   The minor pentatonic scale

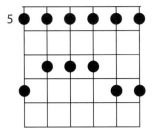

We'll learn the pentatonic scale in its movable form with closed left-hand fingering. Once you learn this fingering pattern you'll be able to play this scale in any key, anywhere on the neck.

The fingering for the pentatonic scale works the same way as the blues scale: If you start again on the fifth fret, all notes on that fret will be played by the first finger. In this scale there are no notes on the sixth fret. All notes on the seventh fret will be played by the third finger, and all notes on the eighth fret will be played by the fourth finger.

Practice this scale forward and backward, beginning on the fifth fret. Once you have that down, move the scale to other parts of the neck. When you move the scale down toward the headstock you'll have the challenge of stretching your fingers a little more to reach the notes. When you move it up toward the body of the guitar you'll have the challenge of fitting your fingers cleanly into smaller spaces on the fingerboard.

If you'd rather not buy a physical metronome, check out some alternatives on the Internet. There are some software versions of metronomes that you can run directly from your computer. Check out the freely downloadable PC shareware "KeepTime" at www.audioplayer.com/smm/programs/KeepTime/download.shtml or the Macintosh software "Drone" at www.audioplayer.com/smm/programs/Drone/download.shtml.

Scales are one of the best ways to develop coordination, strength, and agility in your fingers. They can seem boring at times, but you can make them sound better and be more interesting for you by doing one thing—treating them as a piece of music instead of just an exercise. When you play the notes of a scale, give each one attention and put some emotion into it. That's how you'll want your music to sound.

Introduction to the 12-Bar Blues

Now let's take a look at the most basic blues chord progression, the 12-bar blues (**Figure 5–3**). We'll learn this progression in the key of A, to go along with the blues scale and the pentatonic scale that you just learned.

Figure 5–3   12-bar blues progression

ELSEWHERE ON THE WEB

▶ Did you know that *B.B.* stands for "Blues Boy," and that the blues legend's first name is actually Riley? This and much more information about America's Ambassador of the Blues can be found on John Babich's About.com blues Web site. Just go to http://about.com/blues/bbkinginfo.

Figure 5–4   8-bar blues progression

In this progression each bar has four beats (counted 1-2-3-4). Let's use the first strumming pattern that you learned in Chapter 4: the pattern that has eight strums per bar (counted "1 and 2 and 3 and 4 and"), with the downstrokes on the numbers and the upstrokes on the *and*s. The chords on the chart are all major. As you play, watch the chart to follow which bar you're on so you know when to change chords. When you get to the end of the last bar, just go right back to the first bar and continue without stopping.

For the sake of simplicity, this 12-bar blues is presented in a very basic, almost "hokey" style. Learn it as is for now so you become familiar with the form. We'll vary the style in upcoming chapters to make the blues sound more interesting.

Other Blues Progressions

The 12-bar blues is just one of many possible blues progressions. Another one that's used quite often is the **8-bar blues**. The chords are all major (**Figure 5–4**).

Each bar has four beats. We'll use the same strumming pattern to play this progression as we did for the 12-bar blues. When you get to the end of the last bar, just go right back to the first bar and continue without stopping.

Figure 5–5   16-bar blues progression 1

While the 8-bar blues condenses the blues progression into its most compact form, the **16-bar blues** expands on the blues progression and takes it through new twists and turns. Let's switch to the key of E for the next two blues progressions, just to reorient our ears.

This 16-bar blues progression (**Figure 5–5**) is like the 12-bar blues, but in the 16-bar form the second line is repeated.

In order to play a blues progression in E we're going to need a new chord—B major (**Figure 5–6**).

The fingering of the B major chord is very close to the A major chord when it's fingered with the second, third, and fourth fingers. To form the B major chord you simply slide that A major chord up two frets and place your first finger on the second fret of the first string. To move from the B to the A in bars 13 and 14, just lift your first finger off the first string and slide your second, third, and fourth fingers down two frets.

Here's a strum variation that breaks up the repetitiveness of the strum we're using now—we'll add **accents** to beat 1 and the *and* of beat 2 of our strums. Adding an accent to a strum means that you hit that strum harder than the rest of your strums to emphasize it. The accent pattern looks like this, accenting on the bold:

1-and-2-**and**-3-and-4-and

You can use this accent pattern on every bar of the progression.

This next 16-bar blues progression takes a different direction in the seventh and eighth bars, and in the **turnaround** (the last four bars). Try this progression with the straight strumming pattern and the accented pattern—it sounds good with both of them (**Figure 5–7**).

These additional blues progressions, along with the 12-bar blues, make a good introduction to the many variations of the blues. Try playing them at different **tempos** or speeds. Blues progressions are played at every tempo, from extremely slow ones (like "Summertime") to breakneck ones (like "Twenty Flight Rock"). Finally, remember to put feeling into it every time that you practice your blues progressions.

What I mean when I say "put feeling" into your progressions is that you should not just play them like an exercise in which you focus entirely on the motions and techniques you need to

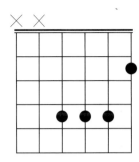

Figure 5–6   B major chord

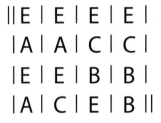

Figure 5–7   16-bar blues progression 2

	E	E	E	E
A	A	C	C
E	E	B	B
A	C	E	B	

physically make the progressions happen. That's important, but it's just as important to focus on the emotions you're trying to communicate when you're playing music. When you think of those emotions while you're playing—whether you're playing a slow, sad blues or a very fast, high-energy, and positive one—they get communicated through your instrument. So play your progressions as if they were songs rather than exercises.

Introduction to B.B. King's Guitar Style

One great thing about B.B. King's music is its simplicity. As cool as his guitar playing sounds, the truth is that King's basic solo style is pretty easy to learn. Besides the actual notes that B.B. King plays, which we'll discuss shortly, there are a few major concepts that define B.B. King's guitar work—particularly his **phrasing** and his unique **vibrato**.

The first concept to tackle when trying to learn to play blues in a B.B. King style is how to "phrase" your solos. To understand what phrasing means, think of the way you talk—you form ideas into sentences, and at the end of each sentence you pause. B.B. King plays guitar the same way. He plays one idea and then pauses at the end of that phrase, before continuing on with his next idea.

Because most guitarists like to play long streams of notes more than they like to stop playing notes, this may be a difficult concept to master at first. Practice playing five or six notes, then pausing for a few seconds, then continuing with a new series of notes. Concentrate on making each of these short riffs sound complete, and try to make your series of notes sound resolved at the end, as if your "sentence" is over. This may be a little overwhelming at first, but as you continue to practice, your phrasing skills will grow stronger and stronger.

Mastering the highly individual sounding vibrato of B.B. King will also take some practice. While some guitarists use only their fingers to create vibrato, B.B. uses his whole hand, rapidly rocking the string back and forth across the fingerboard. Listen to King's guitar playing, and try to mimic his vibrato sound. Notice that although B.B.'s vibrato is very pronounced, he doesn't use it all the time. King reserves vibrato for notes that are held for longer periods of time, or notes he wants to accentuate.

Now let's take a look at B.B. King's fretting hand position. If you've had some experience playing blues guitar, chances are if I said "let's play a blues in A," your hand would automatically slide to the fifth fret of your guitar, the standard A blues scale position. That's cool—you can certainly play a lot of great guitar licks in that position, but you should know it's not a position that B.B. King uses much. King favors a different area of the guitar fingerboard—he places his first finger on the second string root note. So, if you were playing a B.B. style guitar solo in the key of A, you'd look for the note A on the second string (10th fret), and position your first finger on that fret. It is important to note that, even though the chords in the song change, B.B. will generally use this position as his "home base," slightly varying the notes he selects in that position to fit the different chords.

Not familiar with the notes on the second string yet? That's OK, but if you want to start playing like B.B., now's the time to learn them, and learn them well. To set your landmarks, the open second string and the 12th fret are the note B, the 5th fret is E, and the 10th fret is A. Using these landmarks you'll quickly be able to find the proper root note you're looking for.

Find the root note now. We'll play in the key of A, so find A on the second string. Fret the note with your first finger, and play it. Now, play it again. And again. Get used to it—B.B. likes to keep his phrases simple, and you'll hear him coming back to this root note constantly.

Take a look at **Figure 5–8**. These are the frets, centered around the root (shown in red), that B.B. plays extensively. King will bend many of these notes, however, to raise their pitch to a higher note. In the key of A, for example, B.B. likes to play the 2nd string, 12th fret (the note above the root in the diagram) with his third finger, which he immediately bends up to the 14th fret. He'll often follow that note with the root note, the 10th fret on the second string (with a healthy dollop of vibrato, of course). Give it a try.

Figure 5–8   B.B.'s favorite notes

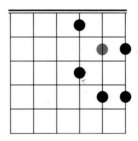

B.B. often plays the lowest note in the above diagram with his second finger, which he then slides up two frets to play the other note on the third string. Then he'll end this mini-riff with the root on the second string, held with vibrato. This is a common B.B. phrase, one you'll hear in almost every solo he plays. Try this one too.

Another favorite B.B. lick is playing the highest note in the pattern (in the key of A it would be 12th fret on the first string), then bending it up two frets. From there, King will often return the string to its unbent position, replay the same fret, and end the lick with (you guessed it) the root. Take a few minutes to add this riff to your repertoire.

Perhaps the most important lesson to take away from these phrases is King's interest in playing the root. Most of his blues riffs end on the root, and yours should too. This gives the riff a satisfying feeling of resolution.

In addition to the above, you'll want to learn where the root is, one octave up, on the first string, which is on the 17th fret—B.B. likes to slide up to this note at the climax of the solo.

More Signature B.B. King Guitar Phrases

Let's look at a few more of B.B. King's distinctive guitar riffs. The B.B. King blues guitar transcriptions we'll talk about now are in the key of A, so, as before, we'll get into B.B. position with our first finger centered on the root note A on the second string (10th fret).

Start by going to my About.com site: http://about.com/guitar/playlikebb1. The first tab excerpt is just a quick little riff by B.B., on the tune "There's Something on Your Mind" (with Etta James), from his 1993 album *Blues Summit.*

This is a simple but classic B.B. King lick. You'll hear King play variations on this riff in virtually every solo he's ever played. Familiarize yourself with this pattern, and try to match the vibrato and bend exactly.

You can listen to an MP3 file of this phrase on my About.com site: http://about.com/guitar/audiotheressomethingonyourmind.

Now scroll down the page to the next solo tab. This is an excerpt from the middle of a 12-bar blues called "Worry, Worry" from one of King's most highly regarded albums, 1964's *Live at the Regal,* a must-own album for blues guitar fans.

This tab is a prime example of the B.B. position. King stays in this position on the neck for the entire transcribed solo. Notice all the different sounds he gets out of his guitar by varying how far he bends notes, and by sliding and adding vibrato. This is the longest and most complicated tab we've looked at, so take your time learning this solo, and memorize the entire passage. Try to get your playing as smooth and flowing as B.B.'s.

ASK YOUR GUIDE

How do I use my movable blues scale when we change keys to E?

▶ When we were playing the movable blues scale in the key of A we started on the fifth fret of the sixth string—which is the note A. That's because the root of this scale is the first note on the sixth string. Therefore, when you want to move this movable scale to another key, you simply aim for that note on the sixth string. To play lead guitar over progressions in the key of E, move your blues scale up the neck so that it begins on the twelfth fret, which is marked on most guitars with a double dot on the fingerboard.

It will really help if you can listen to this being played. You can listen to an MP3 file of this solo on my About.com site: http://about.com/guitar/audioworryworry.

Now we'll shift to some of B.B. King's riffs in the key of C. The next blues guitar transcription is in the key of C, so we'll need to get into B.B. position—with our first finger centered on the root note C on the second string (13th fret). Your other fingers should be poised above the fingerboard, ready to be used at any time.

Go to http://about.com/guitar/playlikebb2. The first tab you'll see features B.B. in one of the more aggressive moods I've ever heard him in. The song is "Stormy Monday," and the form is a traditional 12-bar blues.

King starts the solo with the root note C high up on the fingerboard of the first string (20th fret). Here's another example of why it's important to know where the root of the key is on the first string—B.B. likes to play this note, and slide off of it, in the climax of his solos.

From there, it's back to the standard B.B. position, in which King plays some of his favorite riffs, plus a few other phrases we don't hear him play quite as often. King executes some tough first finger bends, which we'll see more of in following transcriptions. You'll need to spend some time on this solo to get everything sounding connected, and once you do you'll have some excellent blues riffs under your belt.

This solo sounds great. You can listen to an MP3 file of this solo on my About.com site: http://about.com/guitar/audiostormymonday.

Finally, we'll shift to some of B.B. King's riffs in the key of G. The next B.B. King blues guitar transcription is in the key of G, so, like before, we'll get into B.B. position—with our first finger centered on the root note G on the second string (at the 8th fret).

Go to http://about.com/guitar/playlikebb3. The tab you'll see here features B.B. playing one chorus of 12-bar blues as an introduction to the song "Good Man Gone Bad," from his 1998 album *Blues on the Bayou.*

There are lots of vintage King licks here—including some tricky passages that sound deceptively simple. Twice during this tab, B.B. uses his first finger to bend a note on the first string. The first time the note is bent up a half step, and the second time the note is bent up a whole step. This can be tough to execute, and it will require some practice in order to get your first finger strong enough for these whole step bends.

As always, B.B. uses short phrases with lots of space between them. When you've mastered this solo, try playing a solo in a similar style, but with different notes, along with the MP3.

Listening will really help you get a feel for this solo. You can listen to an MP3 file of this solo on my About.com site: http://about .com/guitar/audiogoodmangonebad.

If you devote some serious time you should quickly learn the basic style and sound of B.B. King's guitar style. If you want the best shot at learning and assimilating King's guitar techniques, I recommend that you spend time listening to and playing along with his albums.

New Strumming Pattern

I hope you've been practicing your strumming patterns from Chapter 4. The more you play them the more natural they'll feel, and the less you'll have to think about them as you play your progressions.

Let's look at our next variation on the basic strumming pattern. In the last variation we deviated from the basic pattern by dropping out the fifth strum. In this new pattern we'll drop out both the second and the fifth strums (**Figure 5–9**). You can listen to an MP3 file of this strumming pattern on my About.com site: http://about. com/guitar/audiostrum3. Take some time to get the rhythm locked in your head. The sample is long enough to play along with too, so try playing along with it using a G major chord. Once you get familiar with it, listen to the other MP3 file of the strum at a faster speed (http://about.com/guitar/audiostrum3fast), and try playing along with that.

Figure 5–9   Strumming pattern

We'll use the same strumming technique that we used for the previous pattern. Keep the up-and-down strumming motion going on the 1-and-2-and-3-and-4-and count, using downstrokes on the numbers and upstrokes on the *ands*. When you get to the second and fifth strums in the pattern, which occur on the *and* of the 1 and 3 counts, just lift the pick away from the strings and "miss" them with the strums. Then lower the pick again so you're on the strings with the next strum.

Be sure to use the exact upstrokes and downstrokes that are indicated on the strum notation. You can check yourself by thinking of the strum in downstrokes and upstrokes. The motion with your strumming arm and wrist would be down-up-down-up-down-up-down-up, but the strums you would actually strike with your pick would be down, down-up, up-down-up. Try saying that out loud as you play the pattern. Remember the following important points as you practice.

- Make sure to strum directly over the sound hole.
- Make sure all the strings are ringing clearly.
- Make sure the volume of your downstrokes and upstrokes are equal.
- Be careful not to strum too hard, as this often causes strings to buzz or rattle.
- Be careful not to strum too softly. Your pick should be striking the strings with a relatively firm, even stroke.
- Think of your elbow as being the top of a pendulum; your arm should swing up and down from it in a steady motion, never pausing at any time.
- Though your arm provides the swing, the bulk of the picking motion should come from a rotation of the wrist, rather than from the forearm. Do not keep your wrist stiff.

Songs You Can Play Now

With ten chords under your belt and the blues on your mind, I'm sure you'll want to practice songs based on blues progressions this week.

- ○ "Johnny B. Goode," *Chuck Berry*
  www.chordie.com/chord.pere/www.lindesign.se/uwp/guitar/b/
  chuck_berry/johnny_b_goode.crd

- ○ "Key to the Highway," *Eric Clapton version*
  www.chordie.com/chord.pere/getsome.org/guitar/olga/
  chordpro/c/Eric.Clapton/KeyToTheHighWay.chopro

- ○ "Sweet Little Sixteen," *Chuck Berry*
  www.chordie.com/chord.pere/www.ultimate-guitar.com/print
  .php?what=tab&id=16995

I hope you're putting in your fifteen minutes of practice time per day! That's not a lot of time to play guitar, but even fifteen

◄◄◄
Here are three songs you can try that include all three kinds of blues progressions you learned. "Johnny B. Goode" is a 12-bar blues, "Key to the Highway" is an 8-bar blues, and "Sweet Little Sixteen" is (you guessed it!) a 16-bar blues.

minutes a day will yield good results over time. If you're inclined to play more, I highly encourage you to do so!

Here's a list of how to spend your daily practice time:

1. Make sure your guitar is in tune.
2. Warm up by playing the blues scale forward and backward, several times. Play slowly using alternate picking, and make sure each note rings clearly.
3. Review all ten chords we've learned. Practice moving from one chord to another quickly.
4. Spend some time practicing this week's new strumming pattern. Also, be sure to practice the two strumming patterns from Chapter 4. Try switching from one chord to another while using these strumming patterns, always making your chord change on the first beat of the pattern.
5. Try to play one or more of the songs listed in this chapter. See if you can memorize part of a song, including the lyrics. At this point the songs may not come out as strongly as you'd hope, but be patient. You'll be sounding like a pro within months!

If practicing everything on this list seems overwhelming in one sitting, it's okay to break up the material and practice it over several days. Make sure you get through the whole list, though, before going back to the beginning. There is a strong human tendency to practice only the things that we are already good at. You need to overcome this, and force yourself to practice the things you are weakest at doing.

The key to becoming a good guitarist is to enjoy practicing and playing guitar. The more you enjoy playing, the more you'll want to pick up your guitar. If you find yourself getting overly frustrated, put the guitar down, and go do something else. Come back to practicing later. Don't put too much pressure on yourself—you shouldn't expect to sound great at this point. In fact, you should think of anything you've accomplished thus far as a bonus. If you think back to what you sounded like when you first picked up the instrument, I'm sure you'll realize that you've already improved immensely.

Get Linked

*You can find more information on the subjects we've discussed in this chapter on my **About.com** site. Check out this helpful link.*

BLUES GUITAR LEGENDS

This site spotlights Robert Johnson, T. Bone Walker, B.B. King, and Albert King.

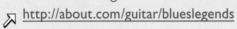 http://about.com/guitar/blueslegends

Chapter 6

Learning the Notes

The Musical Alphabet

Up until now, we've spent most of our time focused on the bottom few frets of the guitar. All of the chords you've learned are in the **open position**, which means all the notes in the chords are either open strings or are fretted within the first four frets of the fingerboard. And, except for some of the blues tab we just looked at, the farthest we've reached up the fingerboard has been to the eighth fret, the highest fret we got to when we played the blues scale or the pentatonic scale in fifth position (starting on the fifth fret).

Most guitars have at least nineteen frets, so you can see there's a large area of the fingerboard that we haven't begun to explore yet. In this chapter we'll start learning the notes all over the fingerboard, which is the first step we need to take in order to unlock the instrument's full potential.

Before we begin learning notes, let's take a moment to understand how the "musical alphabet" works. It uses the first seven letters of the alphabet—A, B, C, D, E, F, G—and starts over again on A.

Figure 6–1   The musical alphabet

E⁀F   G   A   B⁀C   D   E⁀F   G   A . . . .

When you get to that second A you've reached the same note one **octave** higher than the original A you started with, which is the same note at twice the **frequency** or number of **beats per second (bps)**. For example, the open A string on the guitar vibrates at a frequency of 110 bps. The A one octave higher, played by fretting the twelfth fret on the A string, vibrates at a frequency of 220 bps.

Take a look at the illustration of the musical alphabet (**Figure 6–1**). The **interval** or space between most of the notes in the scale is a **whole step**, which means that the second note is two frets higher than the first note. But there are two places in the scale where the interval between the notes is a **half step**, meaning that the second note is just one fret higher than the first. These two places are illustrated by the ties between the notes in **Figure 6–1**. They occur between B and C, and between E and F.

This rule applies to all instruments, including piano. If you are familiar with the piano keyboard, you will know that there is no black key between the notes B and C or between E and F. Between all other consecutive notes there is a black key.

On the guitar, there is one fret between all of the notes except between B and C and between E and F. Keep this rule in mind as we learn the notes on the sixth and fifth strings.

Notes on the E and A Strings

The name of the open sixth string is E. Let's figure out the other note names on the sixth string.

Coming after E in the musical alphabet is, of course, F. Because there is no fret between these two notes, we know that F will be on the first fret. We know that there is a fret between F and G, so G will be found on the third fret. Since there is a fret between G and A, the A is on the fifth fret of the sixth string. Continue this process all the way up the sixth string. You can check **Figure 6–2** to make sure you are correct. Remember—there's also no fret between the notes B and C.

Once you reach the twelfth fret (which is often marked on the neck of the guitar by double dots), you'll notice that you have reached E again. On all six strings, the note on the twelfth fret is the same as the open string.

Now try the same process to find the notes on the fifth, or A, string. You'll be looking for the notes B, C, D, E, F, and G, and the octave A. Locate these notes by using the rule about which are a whole step apart and which are only a half step apart, and then check yourself against **Figure 6–2**.

This process works exactly the same way on the other four strings. Just start with the open string name, and then think of the next seven notes in the musical alphabet that you'll be looking for. Finally, use the whole step / half step rule to find those notes. When you get to the twelfth fret you should always be naming the same note as the open string you started on.

Now that you understand how to figure out the names of the notes on the fingerboard, the next step is to memorize them so that you can find them quickly without having to go through the whole process of locating them. For now just memorize the notes on the sixth and fifth strings. Use **Figure 6–2** as an aid in this process.

The best way to go about memorizing the entire fingerboard is to start with several of the note names and frets on each string. If you know where A is on the sixth string, for example, it will be much easier to find B.

In the next chapter we'll look at the names of all the notes in between the notes we're learning now. You will learn about **sharps**

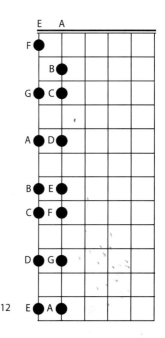

Figure 6–2   The notes on the E and A strings

Figure 6–3   Power chord
on the sixth string

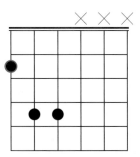

and flats, which are notes a half step higher or a half step lower than the note named. Understanding and learning to name the notes we've discussed here will make finding the sharps and flats easy for you. Things to remember:

- The musical alphabet goes from A to G, then back to A again.
- There are no frets between the notes B and C, or between E and F.
- The note name on the twelfth fret of any string is always the same as the open string.
- Memorize the open string name, and several more note names and locations on both the sixth and fifth string. This will make finding all other notes much quicker.

Fifth Chords: Feel the Power

The time you spent memorizing the notes on the sixth and fifth strings will come in very handy now as we learn about **power chords**.

In some styles of music, particularly in rock and roll, it's not always necessary to play a big, full-sounding chord. Sometimes it sounds better to play chords that are made of just two or three notes. This is when power chords come in handy.

The power chord contains only two different notes: the **root** note (which is the first note of the scale the chord is based on), and a note called the "fifth" because it is the fifth note of the scale that begins with the root. (The third note in the chord diagrammed in **Figure 6–3**, on the fourth string, is the same note as the root, one octave higher.) For this reason, power chords are referred to as **fifth chords** (written C5 or E5, and so on). The power chord does not contain a "third," the note that traditionally tells us whether a chord is major or minor. Therefore, a power chord is neither major nor minor, and it can be used in situations where either a major or a minor chord is called for.

Note that the chord diagram has *X*s above the third, second, and first strings, meaning that you don't play them. If those strings are allowed to ring as you play your power chords, they'll mess up the sound of the chords.

Play the chord by placing your first finger on the sixth string of the guitar. Your third finger should be placed on the fifth string, two frets up from your first finger. Then your fourth finger goes on the fourth string, on the same fret as your third finger. Strum the three notes with your pick, making sure that all three notes ring clearly, and that they're all equal in volume.

The root of the power chord is the note that you're playing on the sixth string with your first finger. Power chords are **movable chords** meaning that, unlike the chords you've learned up to now, you can play them anywhere on the neck. Whatever note your first finger is on defines the name of the chord. For example, if the power chord were being played starting on the fifth fret of the sixth string, it would be referred to as an A power chord, since the note on the fifth fret of the sixth string is A. If the chord were played on the eighth fret, it would be a C power chord. This is why it's so important to know the names of the notes on the sixth string of the guitar.

Try playing this chord progression in open position:

C major–A minor–D minor–G major

If we want to play this chord progression using power chords, we'd play it like this:

C5–A5–D5–G5

To play this progression, start with the power chord with the root (played by your first finger) on the eighth fret. Then slide the

ELSEWHERE ON THE WEB

▶ To see how the notes are arranged on the piano keyboard, as well as what the frequency of each note is, take a look at engineer Tom Irvine's interesting Web site, Vibrationdata.com. (The notes of the open guitar strings on this diagram are E2, A2, D3, G3, B3, and E4.) He covers the music theory behind string vibration, going all the way back to Pythagoras, the Greek mathematician and philosopher who discovered that if you divide the length of a string in half, you get the octave of the original note. Just go to www.vibrationdata.com/piano.htm.

**Figure 6–4   Power chord
on the fifth string**

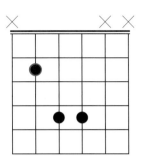

**Figure 6–5   Strumming
pattern #4**

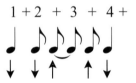

chord down to the fifth fret. Next slide the chord up to the tenth fret, and finally slide it down to the third fret.

Play each of the four chords for one bar (counted 1-2-3-4) using the basic strumming pattern 1-and-2-and-3-and-4-and, with the numbers being downstrokes and the *ands* being upstrokes. Remember to only strum the three strings you're fretting.

Many guitarists prefer to use all downstrokes instead of alternate strumming when playing power chords. This results in a more "chunky" sound, characterized by a strong repeated downstroke that emphasizes the sixth string followed by a short, solid sustain. Give it a try and listen to the difference.

Power chords can also be played starting on the fifth string (**Figure 6–4**).

Now that you can play power chords on the sixth string, making this transition should be no trouble at all. The shape is exactly the same, only this time you'll need to be sure you don't play the sixth string. Many guitarists will overcome this problem by lightly touching the tip of the first finger against the sixth string, deadening it so it doesn't ring.

The root of this chord is on the fifth string, so you'll need to know the notes on this string in order to know what power chord you're playing. If, for example, you're playing a fifth-string power chord on the fifth fret, you are playing a D power chord. If you're playing it on the seventh fret, you are playing an E power chord.

Things you should know about power chords:

- A power chord is also often referred to as a "fifth" or "5" chord. If, for example, you see a chord written as "C5," this is a C power chord.
- You can optionally omit the fourth finger, and play a power chord simply as a 2-note chord. Most guitarists stick with the 3-note version, because it has a fuller sound.

- Another common fingering for a power chord is to play the root note with the first finger, while the third finger **barres** the other two notes, meaning that the third finger covers both the fifth and the fourth strings.
- Power chords are generally used in pop, rock, and blues music. Because they are rather small chords, they are not commonly used in acoustic strumming situations.

New Strumming Pattern

Let's look at our next variation on the basic strumming pattern (**Figure 6–5**).

- In the first variation (pattern #2) we deviated from the basic pattern by dropping the fifth strum.
- In the second variation (pattern #3) we dropped both the second and the fifth strums.
- In this new variation we'll drop the second, fifth, and eighth strums.

You can listen to an MP3 file of this strumming pattern on my About.com site: http://about.com/guitar/audiostrum4. Take some time to get the rhythm locked in your head. The sample is long enough to play along with too, so try playing along with it using a G major chord. Once you get familiar with it, listen to the MP3 file of the strum at a faster speed (http://about.com/guitar/audiostrum4fast), and try playing along with that.

We'll use the same strumming technique that we used for the previous pattern. Keep the up-and-down strumming motion going on the 1-and-2-and-3-and-4-and count, using downstrokes on the numbers and upstrokes on the *and*s. When you get to the second, fifth, and eighth strums in the pattern, which occur on the *and* of the 1-count, on the 3-count, and on the *and* of the 4-count, just lift

ASK YOUR GUIDE

Where did power chords come from?

▶ Power chords have been popular since the birth of blues music. They were easy to play and had a neutral sound that sounded good whether being sung over in a major or a minor key. Rock and roll, a musical form that grew out of the blues, continued the trend of using power chords frequently in progressions. When grunge music started to rise in popularity, many bands chose to use power chords almost exclusively, preferring their tight, focused sound to more "traditional" chord sounds. Today they're mainstays of blues, pop, rock, metal, and alternative rock.

the pick away from the strings and "miss" them with their strums. Then lower the pick again so you're on the strings with the next strum.

Be sure to use the exact upstrokes and downstrokes that are indicated on the strum notation. You can check yourself by thinking of the strum in downstrokes and upstrokes. The motion with your strumming arm and wrist would be down-up-down-up-down-up-down-up, but the strums you would actually strike with your pick would be down, down-up, up-down. Try saying that out loud as you play the pattern.

This is a very common, usable strumming pattern. In fact, many guitarists actually find this strum to be slightly easier than others, because there is a slight pause at the end of the bar, which can be used to switch chords.

Things to remember:

- Make sure to strum directly over the sound hole.
- Make sure all the strings are ringing clearly.
- Make sure the volume of your downstrokes and upstrokes are equal.
- Be careful not to strum too hard, as this often causes strings to buzz or rattle.
- Be careful not to strum too softly either, as this will produce a "wimpy" sound. Your pick should be striking the strings with a relatively firm, even stroke.
- Think of your elbow as being the top of a pendulum; your arm should swing up and down from it in a steady motion, never pausing at any time.
- Though your arm provides the swing, the bulk of the picking motion should come from a rotation of the wrist, rather than from the forearm. Do not keep your wrist stiff when strumming.

Songs You Can Play Now

Now that we've covered all the basic open chords and power chords, we have a lot of options in terms of songs we can play.

○ "Smells Like Teen Spirit," *Nirvana*
www.geocities.com/SunsetStrip/Garage/4564/Smells%5FLike%5FTeen%5FSpirit.txt

○ "Have You Ever Seen the Rain," *Creedence Clearwater Revival*
www.chordie.com/chord.pere/teman.com/guitarz/TABs/c/CCR/HaveYouEverSeenTheRain.chopro

○ "Still Haven't Found What I'm Looking For," *U2*
www.chordie.com/chord.pere/getsome.org/guitar/olga/chordpro/u/U2/StillHaventFound.chopro

○ "Mother," *Pink Floyd*
www.chordie.com/chord.pere/www.pinkfloyd-co.com/band/tab/wall/tab_wall-mother.txt

◄◄◄
These songs focus on both open and power chords. For "Smells Like Teen Spirit," ignore the tablature for now—we'll get to that later—and just focus on the chords for the verses and the chorus. You can use "Mother" to practice your F major chord.

The further we progress in these lessons, the more important it becomes for you to have daily practice time. We've covered a lot now, and we're starting to go over some tricky material, so it might be time to start practicing for half an hour a day if you're not doing so already. Here's a list of how to spend your daily practice time:

1. Make sure your guitar is in tune.
2. Warm up by playing the chromatic scale, forward and backward, several times. Play slowly, use alternate picking, and make sure each note rings clearly.
3. Review the names of the notes on the sixth and fifth strings. Try calling out a random note (such as C), and

then try to find that note on both the sixth and the fifth strings. Memorize at least two other notes, and their positions on each string.

4. Work on your power chords. Power chords can take a while to get used to, so I suggest making a habit of playing them regularly. Make sure your third finger is positioned well on the appropriate fret (this is the finger that most often makes power chords sound bad). Try sliding from chord to chord, and try moving from the sixth-string chords to the fifth-string chords.

5. Review all ten major and minor chords you've learned. You should really be close to memorizing all of these chords by now. Pick two chords, and practice moving from one to the next quickly and smoothly. Then pick two other chords, and repeat the process.

6. Spend some time working on this chapter's new strumming pattern (#4). Also, be sure to revisit patterns 1, 2, and 3 from the previous chapters. Try switching from chord to chord while strumming these patterns.

7. Work on playing that pesky F major chord. Don't give up until it sounds perfect. Try playing the Pink Floyd song "Mother," but use the fingering you learned for the F major chord instead of the full barre version of the chord that's shown on the chord chart (you'll learn that soon).

8. Try to play all of the songs in the list. Each was chosen to help you work on a particular aspect of your guitar playing, so even though they are fun to play, they will also sneak in techniques that will help you improve greatly.

I can't emphasize strongly enough that it is important to practice everything you've learned in these four lessons. Some things will undoubtedly be more fun than others, but trust me, the things you hate doing today are probably techniques that will become the basis for other things you will love to play in the future. The key to practice is, of course, to have fun. The more you enjoy playing guitar, the more you'll play and the better you'll get. Try to have fun with whatever you're playing.

If you find it impossible to find the time to practice everything in one sitting, just break up the material, and practice it over several days. There is a strong human tendency to practice only the things that we are already quite good at. You need to overcome this and force yourself to practice the things you are weakest at doing. Make them your strongest instead!

Get Linked

You can find more information on the subjects we've discussed in this chapter on my **About.com** *site. Check out these helpful links.*

TIPS ON PLAYING FOR A CROWD

Those first times playing in front of a crowd can be intimidating. Pull it off like a pro with these helpful tips.

↗ http://about.com/guitar/playingforacrowd

THE IMPORTANCE OF WARMING UP

Avoid repetitive strains injuries with these warm up tips.

↗ http://about.com/guitar/warmingup

Chapter 7

Reading Guitar Tablature

Sharps and Flats

In the last chapter you learned the names of notes on the sixth and fifth strings, but as you remember, we left quite a few frets unidentified.

By now you should know the names of the notes in red in **Figure 7–1** (see following page), but you probably won't recognize the names of the notes in between the red dots. We'll fill in those gaps now.

Let's start by learning two new terms used to describe notes: *sharp* and *flat*. Each one has a symbol—sharp is represented by ♯, while flat is represented by ♭. The term *sharp* means that a note is raised by one fret, an interval also known as a *half step* or a *semitone*. The term *flat* means that a note is lowered by one fret, making it a half step lower.

You'll notice in **Figure 7–1** that each of the in-between notes has two names, one being a letter name followed by a sharp sign, and the other being a letter name followed by a flat sign. That's because

Figure 7–1   Fingerboard with all notes on E and A strings identified

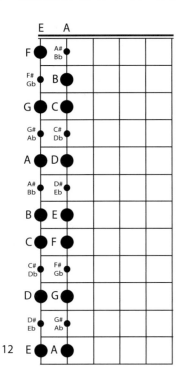

each of these notes can be named as it relates to the note below it or to the note above it. For example, let's focus on the second fret of the sixth string. This note is one fret above the F on the first fret, so we could call it an F sharp (F♯). It is also one fret below the G on the third fret, so we could call it G flat (G♭). Whether you see this note referred to as F♯ or G♭, it's the exact same note.

Things to remember:

- Sharp is notated as ♯.
- Flat is notated as ♭.
- If a letter name is followed by a sharp (♯), the note is one fret higher than the fret you'd normally play that note on. For example, you play G on the third fret of the sixth string. You play G♯ on the fourth fret of the sixth string.
- If a letter name is followed by a flat (♭), the note is one fret lower than the fret you'd normally play that letter name on. For example, you play D on the tenth fret of the sixth string. You play D♭ on the ninth fret of the sixth string.
- There can be two names for the same note: F♯ = G♭; G♯ = A♭; A♯ = B♭; C♯ = D♭; D♯ = E♭.
- The note name on the twelfth fret of any string is always the same as the open string.
- Memorize the open string name, and several more note names and locations on both the sixth and fifth string. This will make finding all other notes much quicker.

Introduction to the Seventh Chord

So far we've studied major chords, minor chords, and fifth (power) chords. With these basic chords at your disposal you can play hundreds of songs, but we're not going to stop here! There are many other types of chords we haven't looked at yet, each of which has its own unique sound and way of adding color to a chord progression.

In this chapter we'll explore another type of chord, the **seventh chord**, which is also known as a **seven chord**. We'll learn three of these chords in the open position.

Let's begin with a G7 chord (**Figure 7–2**). Start playing the G7 by placing your third finger on the third fret of the sixth string. Then put your second finger on the second fret of the fifth string. Last, place your first finger on the first fret of the first string. Make sure your fingers are nicely curled, and strum all six strings. Be sure to check each string individually to make sure they're all ringing clearly.

Notice that this G7 chord looks quite similar to a G major chord—only one note is different. But the fingering is a completely different shape, because in a G major chord we use the second and first fingers on the sixth and fifth strings, while in the G7 chord we use our third and second fingers on the sixth and fifth strings in order to free up the first finger to reach down to the first fret of the first string. Try switching back and forth from the G major chord to the G7 chord—it's a great exercise for your fretting hand.

Now let's try the C7 chord (**Figure 7–3**). Again, this chord is very close in formation to a C major chord, with only one note being different, but this time the two fingerings are almost identical. Form the normal C major chord by placing your third finger on the third fret of the fifth string, your second finger on the second fret of the fourth string, and your first finger on the first fret of the second string. Now place your fourth finger on the third fret of the third string. Note the X over the sixth string on the C7 diagram. Strum just the bottom five strings, and you're playing a C7.

Finally, we'll play a D7 chord (**Figure 7–4**). Start by placing your second finger on the second fret of the third string. Then place your first finger on the first fret of the second string. Last, put your third finger on the second fret of the first string. The D7 diagram has Xs over the sixth and fifth strings, so strum just the bottom four strings, and you're playing a D7.

Figure 7–2   G7 chord

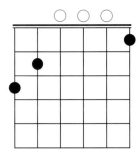

Figure 7–3   C7 chord

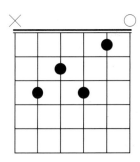

Figure 7–4   D7 chord

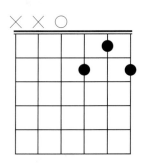

ASK YOUR GUIDE

Should I be learning to sight-read music right now?

▶ There's nothing wrong with taking the more informal approach to learning music. Learning to sight-read takes a reasonable amount of work, without immediate benefit, and this is the sort of duty that self-taught musicians tend to avoid. There are plenty of famous musicians who never learned to read music, so it's not absolutely necessary. That said, if you want to get serious about a career in the music industry, the ability to sight-read will open up opportunities to you that nonreaders wouldn't have a shot at.

As with the previous two chords, you'll notice that the D7 chord is rather similar to the D major chord. But like the G major and the G7, the fingerings are completely different shapes. In a D major chord we use the first and second fingers on the third and first strings, while in the D7 chord we use our third and second fingers on the third and first strings. Things to remember:

- Check each chord you learn for accuracy by playing the strings one at a time. If each string does not ring clearly, find out why, and correct the problem.
- Be sure you're not strumming strings with an X above them in the diagrams. Playing these strings will almost always result in chords sounding wrong.
- Practice moving from chord to chord, saying each chord's name aloud as you're playing it. It is very important to memorize the chord names as well as the chord shapes.

The World of Tablature

Now we're going to explore a system of musical notation that was created by guitarists for guitarists. It's called *guitar tablature,* or **tab**, and it's like a cross between standard musical notation on the staff, and chord or single-note musical diagrams that have fingering indicated. While flawed, tab provides a simple and easy-to-read way of sharing music with other guitarists. Although it may seem complex at first, learning to read tab is quite simple.

Guitarists are a unique breed. Chances are, if you play guitar, you are either self-taught, or you've taken a small number of lessons with a friend or guitar teacher. If you were a pianist, however, you almost assuredly would have learned to play the instrument through years of private study, which would have included both music theory lessons and a heavy focus on **sight-reading**, which is the ability to look at a written page of music and play it immediately.

If you're familiar with reading music you'll immediately notice a few differences between the **standard notation** and tablature. The **tab staff** for guitar has six horizontal lines instead of the five lines of the normal musical staff. It is generally labeled with the letters *TAB* on the left side of the staff to immediately distinguish it from a normal staff. And it has numbers on the staff instead of notes.

Each line on the tab staff represents a string of the instrument. The bottom line of the staff represents your sixth (or lowest E) string; the second line from the bottom represents your fifth (or A) string, and so on, all the way up to the first (or highest E) string on the top of the tab staff. It's essentially a picture of what the strings look like when you look down at them while holding your guitar. That's easy enough to read, right?

Notice that in tablature there are numbers located smack dab in the middle of the lines (a.k.a. strings). The numbers simply represent which fret on that string the tab is telling you to play. For example, in **Figure 7–5** the tab is telling you to play the seventh fret on the third string (third line).

When the letter *0* is used in tablature, this indicates that the open string should be played.

This is the concept of reading tab at its most basic. Now let's examine a more advanced aspect of reading tablature notation—how to read chords in tab.

When the tab displays a series of numbers stacked vertically, like the one above, it's indicating to you that it wants you to play all these notes at the same time. The tablature in **Figure 7–6** indicates that you should hold down the notes in an E major chord (second fret on the fifth string, second fret on the fourth string, first fret on the third string) and strum all six strings at once. Often, tablature will also include the chord name (in this case E major) above the tablature staff, to help guitarists recognize the chord more quickly.

Figure 7–5   Basic tab staff with labeling

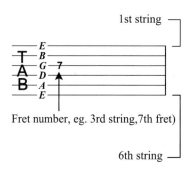

1st string

Fret number, eg. 3rd string, 7th fret)

6th string

Figure 7–6   Tablature for the E major chord (play all notes at once)

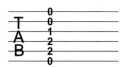

Figure 7–7   E major chord played arpeggio

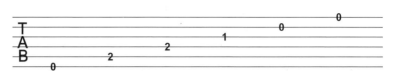

The tablature in **Figure 7–7** contains the same notes as the first E major chord presented in **Figure 7–6**, but because the fret numbers are spread out rather than stacked vertically, it will be played differently. In this situation, the notes in the chord will be played one at a time, rather than all together. "How fast should I play these notes?" you may ask. That's a good question, and one that leads us smoothly into the issue of the fundamental flaws of guitar tab.

The lack of rhythmic notation is the biggest one—and that's a doozy of a flaw! Most guitar tab doesn't notate rhythm in any way, so if you haven't already heard the guitar part to the song you're playing, you have no way of knowing how long to hold each note. Some guitar tab does attempt to include rhythms by putting stems on each number (to indicate quarter notes, eighth notes, and so on from standard notation), but most guitarists find this cumbersome to read. Besides, if you're going to include traditional rhythmic notation in guitar tab, why not just go the extra step and write the whole thing in standard notation?

Another problem with guitar tablature is that only guitarists can read it. Tab is unique to guitarists, so those who don't play guitar won't be able to comprehend it. This can make musical communication with a piano player or other musician difficult. We'll return to guitar tablature as we get into later chapters.

Manipulating the Blues Scale

In Chapter 5 you learned the blues scale. This is an important scale because it plays a central role in rock, pop, and blues music, and it's

ELSEWHERE ON THE WEB

▶ If you want to get a little deeper into reading guitar tab, including looking at a list of the most commonly used symbols in tab that we haven't discussed yet, take a look at this useful Guitar-Consultant.com guide. This Web page also talks about other ways tab can indicate the timing of notes besides adding stems. Just go to: www.guitarconsultant.com/readtablature.html.

used extensively in all styles of guitar solos. Let's take some time to review the blues scale and explore it a little further.

The blues scale is fingered like this: If we're starting on the fifth fret, all notes on the fifth fret will be played by the first finger. All the notes on the sixth fret will be played by the second finger. All notes on the seventh fret will be played by the third finger. Finally, all notes on the eighth fret will be played by the fourth finger.

The blues scale is a movable scale, and because the root of the scale is the note on the sixth string played by your first finger (shown in red in **Figure 7–8**), the key of the blues scale you're playing depends on which fret you begin with. If you start the scale with your first finger on the fifth fret of the sixth string (the note A), you're playing an A blues scale. If you start the scale with your first finger on the eighth fret of the sixth string (the note C), you're playing a C blues scale. You want to pick the key of blues scale that matches the key of the chord progression you're playing against. That means if you're going to play a blues in G, you would select the G blues scale to base your solo on.

If you're interested in learning to play guitar solos, you'll want to spend a whole lot of time with the blues scale. Many pop, rock, and blues guitarists use the blues scale almost exclusively in their solos.

Once you know all the notes in the blues scale, and you can play it forward and backward, it's time to start experimenting. Try playing some **phrases** (a phrase is a series of a few notes) that jump from one part of the blues scale to another. One example would be playing the first five notes of the scale, then jumping up to the top note of the scale (fourth finger on the first string), and then down to the first finger on the first string. You can try moving from any part of the scale to any other part.

The basic premise of forming a solo is this: You pull a series of notes from the blues scale that sound good together—a phrase—

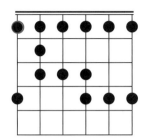

Figure 7–8   The blues scale

and then pull another series of notes from the scale that not only sound good together but also complement or elaborate on the first phrase, and so on. Learning to do this well takes experimentation and practice, but it gets easier and becomes more fun as you go along. Here are some things to try:

- Play the blues scale forward and backward. Try starting in the middle of the scale, and then finishing it, going both forward and backward. In short . . . memorize it well!
- Experiment with playing various notes selected from the A blues scale out of order.
- Play around with the notes in the blues scale, and see if you can't come up with a cool **guitar riff** of your own that could be the basis of a song.

Songs You Can Play Now

On the Eric Clapton song "Wonderful Tonight," you can substitute a regular D major chord for the D/F♯ chord the chart calls for (we'll study these "slash chords" in Chapter 10).

○ "Like a Rolling Stone," *Bob Dylan*
www.geocities.com/etheltheaardvark/like%5Fa%5Frolling%5F stone.txt

○ "Wonderful Tonight," *Eric Clapton*
www.cowboylyrics.com/tabs/kersh-david/wonderful-tonight-4692.html

○ "Other Side," *The Red Hot Chili Peppers*
http://zepperfan.tripod.com/otherside.txt

▶ ▶ ▶
On the Bob Dylan song "Like a Rolling Stone," use this strumming pattern: down, down, down, down-up. You'll see how it fits in with the lyrics. On the Chili Peppers song "Other Side," use this strumming pattern: down, down-up, up-down-up.

I hope that you've increased your daily practice time to half an hour. There are a lot of areas to cover now.

Here's how to spend your daily practice time:

1. Make sure your guitar is in tune.
2. Warm up by playing the blues scale, forward and backward, several times. Play slowly using alternate picking, and make sure each note rings clearly.
3. Play through all the chords you know, including the open chords, power chords, and the seventh chords. Be sure you know the name and shape for each chord.
4. Spend time reviewing the note names on the sixth and fifth string. Memorizing these notes is essential. Start by memorizing a few notes on each string.
5. Review all the strumming patterns we've covered. We've learned four strumming patterns now. Try switching from chord to chord while using each of these patterns.
6. Review the F major chord. It might not sound perfect yet, but chances are, if you've been practicing it, it's getting better and better. Keep it up.
7. Try to play all of the songs listed. Don't get frustrated if a song is too tough for you. Take a deep breath, and try some more. If you're feeling overwhelmed, move to an easier song or try songs from previous lessons.

Remember: Don't just practice your best riffs and chord progressions. It's even more important to practice the things that give you the most trouble. Make your weakest techniques into your strongest techniques and you'll advance quickly.

TOOLS YOU NEED

▶ Many songwriters use parts of the blues scale as the foundation for their songs. For example, Eric Clapton used part of the blues scale for the riff in Cream's song "Sunshine of Your Love." See if you can figure this riff out for yourself—it's one of the most famous in all of rock and roll. Here's a hint: All of the notes in the riff are on the fourth, fifth, or sixth strings of the scale.

If you're feeling confident with everything we've learned so far, find a few songs you're interested in, and try learning them on your own. You can use the guitar tab area of my About.com site to hunt down the music that you'd enjoy learning the most. Try memorizing some of these songs, rather than always looking at the music to play them.

Get Linked

You can find more information on the subjects we've discussed in this chapter on my **About.com** *site. Check out these helpful links.*

**MORE ABOUT
PLAYING SOLOS**

If you have an interest in learning more about soloing, check out this lesson on Learning to Improvise.

↗ http://about.com/guitar/improv

GUITAR TAB LIBRARY

Look on the guitar tab center for new songs to learn.

↗ http://about.com/guitar/tab

Chapter 8

Using the Whole Neck

Introduction to Barre Chords

Every guitarist can remember learning his or her first barre chord—it's a rite of passage that takes you from the realm of beginner into the realm of advanced beginner. That's because learning barre chords frees you from the confines of open position chords and unlocks the potential of the whole neck very rapidly. Think of this—as soon as you can play an A major barre chord, you can also play that same major chord in all eleven other keys simply by moving the exact same chord shape up and down the fingerboard.

You've already taken your first baby step into barre chords with the F major chord. The term *barre* means to hold down two or more strings with the same finger, and as you'll recall, in the F major chord we hold down the second and first strings with the first finger.

Your first finger will take on a whole new role playing barre chords: covering all or most of the strings of the guitar at one time. In the B minor chord your first finger has the job of covering the

Figure 8–1 B minor barre chord

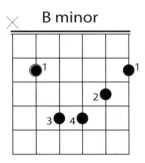

B minor

- root is on the fifth string
- don't play sixth string
- "roll back" first finger
- check notes one string at a time

second fret, from the fifth to first strings (we don't play the sixth string—note the X above it in **Figure 8–1**). Next put your third finger on the fourth fret of the fourth string. Then add your fourth finger to the fourth fret of the third string. Last, place your second finger on the third fret of the second string. Now strum the chord, and try not to freak out when most of the notes don't ring clearly. This is a tough chord to play at first and it's going to take some patience, but it will sound good once you practice it for a while.

Here are some tips that will help:

- Very slightly bend your first finger as you barre the strings. A straight and rigid finger is not what we're looking for.
- Roll the finger back slightly toward the headstock, so that more of the side of your index finger that's closest to your thumb is in contact with the strings.
- Try slightly pulling the body of the guitar toward your body, using the arm of your picking hand. At the same time, gently pull the neck toward you with your fretting hand. This added pressure makes fretting barre chords somewhat easier.

One of the greatest things about the B minor chord shape, and about barre chords in general, is that they are **movable chords**. This means that, unlike the chords you've learned so far, you can slide this exact same shape around to different frets to create different minor chords. In this chord the root is on the fifth string (as indicated in red in **Figure 8–1**), so whatever note your finger is playing on the fifth string is the key of the minor chord you're playing. If you were to slide the chord up the neck, so that your first finger was at the fifth fret, you'd be playing a D minor chord, since the note on the fifth fret of the fifth string is D. Once again, this is why learning the names of the notes on the sixth and fifth strings is so important.

Things to try:

- Hold the shape of the B minor chord, and play the strings one at a time. Correct any notes that aren't ringing clearly.
- Try moving from other chords to a B minor chord, then back to other chords. This will be a slow and difficult process at first. Keep trying!
- Try playing different minor chords by moving the B minor shape around to different frets (for example, try playing C♯ minor, F minor, G minor, B♭ minor, and so on)
- Do NOT play the sixth string when playing a B minor chord. Pay careful attention to this.

More on the Movable Scale

You had your first encounter with a movable scale when we studied the blues scale in Chapter 5. You can play the blues scale in any key you want by selecting that note as your starting point on the sixth string.

Now we'll take a scale you've tried before and learn the movable version of it. The very first scale you learned was the chromatic scale. We studied this scale in the open position, meaning that we used open strings for some of the notes. By contrast, the movable version does not use open strings.

Before we begin, let's review exactly what a chromatic scale is. In Western music, there are twelve different musical pitches (A, B♭, B, C, D♭, D, E♭, E, F, G♭, G, and A♭). The chromatic scale includes every one of these twelve pitches. You could actually play a chromatic scale simply by sliding your finger up one string, playing each fret.

Playing the chromatic scale is a great exercise for improving your finger technique and getting your fretting hand to move smoothly and quickly all over the neck.

ELSEWHERE ON THE WEB

▶ For a little more review on the basics of playing barre chords, have a look at the eHow.com Web page about them. This page takes you step by step through the process with some good tips, and it also includes photos of forming a barre chord that you might find helpful. Just go to www.ehow.com/how_7024_play-barre-chords.html.

**Figure 8–2   Chromatic
scale with closed fingering**

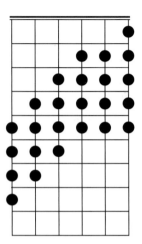

In this scale we play four notes on each string **Figure 8–2**. The picking pattern for each string is down-up-down-up alternate picking. Before you start playing the scale, try practicing just the picking pattern first. Rest the fingers of your fretting hand lightly on the strings to deaden them. Then take your pick and, starting with the sixth string, play each string in succession with the down-up-down-up pattern. Try to keep the rhythm of your plucks even as you change from string to string.

To play the chromatic scale, start by placing your first finger on the fifth fret of the sixth string, and play that note with a down-stroke. Next use your second finger to play the sixth fret of the sixth string (with an upstroke). Then use your third finger to play the seventh fret on the sixth string (with a downstroke). Last, your fourth finger should play the eighth fret (with an upstroke).

Now, move on to the fifth string. Playing this string will require a **position shift** in your fretting hand. Move your hand position down one fret, starting on the fourth fret of the fifth string with your first finger. Play each note on that string, as you did on the sixth. Repeat this process on each of the sixth strings. (Note that you DON'T switch positions going to the second string. This is because the second string is tuned differently than the other five.)

When you reach the first string, do the position shift and play the first fret with your first finger, as usual. Then, immediately shift position up one fret and also play the second fret with your first finger. This step allows you to go up to the fifth fret, thus completing the 2-octave A chromatic scale.

When you've reached the end of the scale, try playing it backward. Things to remember:

- Keep your fretting hand as loose as possible. If you grip the neck too tightly, switching positions will become more difficult.

- Try to set up a steady rhythm while playing the scale. Focus on making it sound as fluid as possible. Play the scale as slowly as necessary in order to make the tempo even throughout. When you've got it, then speed it up.
- Alternate picking is extremely important here. Don't allow yourself to be careless with your picking hand.
- Try looking at your picking hand while you play, instead of at your fretting hand. Is it doing everything as efficiently as it should?
- Don't rush through this exercise, and don't allow yourself to get frustrated. Pay careful attention to any minor flaws in your technique, and try to remedy them.

Barre Chord Basics

Let's get back into these beautiful barre chords. These chords are difficult to play at first, but with practice they will open up whole new worlds in your guitar playing.

You'll notice a new feature in the chord diagram in **Figure 8–3** —the little numbers that tell you which fingers to use to play each note of the chord.

The key to playing this F major shape well is getting your first finger to flatten across the entire fingerboard on the first fret. Try rolling your first finger back slightly toward the headstock of the guitar. Once your first finger feels firmly in place, add your third, fourth, and second fingers to complete the chord. Playing this shape well requires considerable practice, but it will get easier, and soon you won't remember why these shapes ever caused you any problems.

As with the B minor chord you learned, this major chord shape is a movable chord. This means we can slide this chord up and down the neck in order to play major chords in any key. The root of the chord is on the sixth string, so whatever note you are

Figure 8–3   F major barre chord

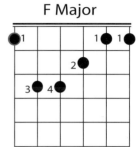

F Major

- root is on the sixth string
- "roll back" first finger
- check notes one string at a time

Figure 8–4   F minor barre chord

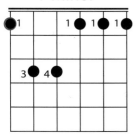

F Minor

- root is on the sixth string
- "roll back" first finger
- make sure third string "rings"
- check notes one string at a time

holding down on the sixth string is the letter name of that major chord. For example, if you were playing the chord at the fifth fret, it would be an A major chord. If you were playing the chord at the second fret, it would be a G♭ major chord (which could also be called F♯ major).

This next chord is very similar to the F major shape (**Figure 8–4**). The only difference is that your second finger is not used at all. This means your first finger is now responsible for fretting four of the six notes in the chord.

Although the F minor chord looks slightly easier to play than the major chord, many guitarists initially have a harder time making the chord sound correct. When playing the chord, pay careful attention to the third string. Is the note ringing clearly? If not, try to correct the problem.

This minor chord is also a movable shape. If you played this chord on the eighth fret, you'd be playing a C minor chord. On the fourth fret, you'd be playing an A♭ minor chord (which could also be called G♯ minor).

Once you get the hang of playing these new shapes, you can start using them everywhere. One of the best ways to practice barre chords is to try using them in songs you already know how to play. To do this, simply use barre chords instead of the open chords you've been using. For example, try playing the song "Leaving on a Jet Plane" using major barre chords. Things to try:

- If you're feeling overwhelmed by getting started with barre chords, try playing any songs you know that use an F major chord. Play all other chords in the song with regular open chord shapes, but use the barre shape for the F major.
- Make a sincere effort to learn the names of the notes on the sixth and fifth string. I can't stress enough how important this is to learn. Knowing the names of the notes on the

sixth and fifth strings is essential to the proper use of barre chords.

- Play barre chords for just a few minutes every day—but do play them every day. You'll be surprised how quickly you learn them.

Introduction to Open Tunings

Despite all of its wonderful characteristics, the guitar does have a few shortcomings. One of these shortcomings is that, because of the way the guitar is laid out, there are chords we can imagine or might have heard that we know would sound great, but that we're unable to play because our human fingers just can't stretch far enough to reach the combination of notes required.

Luckily, there's a way to overcome this problem. By changing the tuning of one or more strings of the guitar, we can play combinations of notes that we previously couldn't. Many of these "**alternate tunings**" or "**open tunings**" have been explored extensively by ambitious musicians—Joni Mitchell claims to have played in 51 different guitar tunings during her career. These alternate tunings open up a whole new world for guitarists willing to look beyond the standard E A D G B E tuning.

Learning to play guitar in many of these new tunings at once can be an overwhelming task. If you thought learning guitar was tricky enough the first time in standard tuning, you're in for a real challenge now! Guitarists have to completely relearn how to play chords for each new tuning they undertake. For this reason, many guitarists tend to explore one alternate tuning for an extended period of time, before they turn their attention to the next.

Let's begin with the alternate tuning known as "**Drop D tuning**." It's one of the most basic open tunings because you only have to change the tuning of one string to create it. Drop D tuning changes the strings to D A D G B E.

ASK YOUR GUIDE

How long will it take me to master barre chords?

▶ Playing these chords well will take time, so don't allow yourself to get frustrated! It took me months to get them to sound as clearly as I liked. The key is getting the pressure on your first finger just right—it has to be just strong enough to get clear tones on all of the strings you're barring, but no harder. If you use too much pressure on your first finger, your fretting hand will hurt and start to cramp quickly.

To get into Drop D tuning, just tune your sixth string down a whole step to D, which is the same note as your fourth string one octave lower.

You can listen to a sound file of this Drop D tuning on my About.com site. Just go to http://about.com/guitar/audiodropd tuning.

Although this tuning has been around for a long time, the Seattle grunge movement in the early 1990s brought about its current popularity. Drop D tuning was used extensively by bands like Nirvana, partly because it made playing power chords with one finger possible. That's because the sixth, fifth, and fourth strings form a natural D5 power chord, so barring those three strings on any fret creates a power chord with root on sixth. (Don't forget, though, that all the notes on your sixth string are a whole step lower when you're looking for a root.)

The best place to begin exploring this tuning is by playing a D major chord in open position and strumming all six strings—you'll hear a giant, resonant chord with the root ringing out in three octaves.

The popular Soundgarden tune "Spoonman" illustrates how you can use one finger to play impressive power chords in drop D tuning. You'll find the tab for it at www.angelfire.com/mi2tabmandu/spoon man.txt.

Now let's move on to another popular open tuning called "**DADGAD tuning**," known as such because this tuning changes the strings to D A D G A D.

To get into DADGAD, start by tuning your sixth string down a whole step to D. Check the tuning against the fourth (D) string. Then tune your second string down a whole step to A. Check the tuning against the fifth (A) string. Lastly, tune your first string down a tone to D. Check the tuning against the fourth (D) string.

You can listen to a sound file of this DADGAD tuning on my About.com site. Just go to http://about.com/guitar/audiodadgadtuning.

This tuning has a beautiful shimmering sound due to the three octaves of Ds and the harmonic tension introduced by the major second interval, the G and A, stuck in between.

More Open Tunings

I hope you're having fun with the open tunings you've learned so far. One of the most exciting things about alternate tunings is the way each one resets your head about what kind of chord sounds are possible to play on the guitar.

Now we'll look at two more open tunings that provide good settings for playing slide guitar, beginning with **Open D tuning**. Open D tuning changes the strings to D A D F♯ A D.

To get into Open D tuning, first tune your sixth string down a whole step to D. Check the tuning with the fourth (D) string. Then tune your third string down a half step to F♯. Check the tuning with the fourth fret of your fourth string. Then tune your second string down a whole step to A. Check the tuning with the fifth (A) string. Finally, tune your first string down a whole step to D. Check the tuning with the fourth (D) string.

You can listen to a sound file of this Open D tuning on my About.com site. Just go to http://about.com/guitar/audioopend tuning.

When the open strings are strummed in this tuning, the sound of a D major chord is produced. This has made this tuning a favorite of slide players, who can simply lay their slide straight across one fret to play chords.

Open D tuning is also played by fingering chords and melodies, so spend some time experimenting with the sound of different finger positions on this tuning.

TOOLS YOU NEED

▶ There is a whole subculture of guitarists who play exclusively in DADGAD tuning, as it lends itself well to certain types of styles. Celtic music is a good example, and there's plenty of it to explore on the DADGAD Tab Archive. In addition to the reels and jigs you'll find polkas, waltzes and other interesting uses for the DADGAD tuning. Just go to http://about.com/guitar/dadgad.

► We haven't discussed how to play slide guitar in any detail yet, but here are a few things you should know about it.

(1) The slide is a tube that fits over one of the fingers on your fretting hand—some people use their third finger, and some use their fourth finger so that the other three fingers are free to play chords.

(2) The slide does not press the strings down against the frets—rather, it slides along the surface of the strings, touching them but not pressing them down.

(3) To play a note in tune the slide must rest directly above the metal fret, not over the space on the fingerboard behind the metal fret.

Let's move on to another open tuning that's great for playing slide guitar, the **Open G tuning**. Open G tuning changes the strings to D G D G B D.

To get into Open G tuning, start by tuning your sixth string down a whole step to D. Check the tuning with the fourth (D) string. Then tune your fifth string down a whole step to G. Check the tuning with the third (G) string. Lastly, tune your first string down a whole step to D. Check the tuning with the fourth (D) string.

You can listen to a sound file of this Open G tuning on my About.com site. Just go to http://about.com/guitar/audioopengtuning.

Keith Richards has always loved this tuning, and has written many classic Rolling Stones riffs in open G. Many slide players also prefer open G, which is tuned to a G major chord.

The classic Rolling Stones riff from "Start Me Up" is played in open G tuning. Note that Keith Richards removed the lowest string from his Telecaster electric guitar for this song (and many others), so the tab only includes notation for the top five strings. Try playing the riff yourself. You can find the tab at www.rockmagic.net/guitar-tabs/rolling-stones/start_me_up.tab.

New Strumming Pattern

We've studied four strumming patterns up to now. If you're comfortable playing those patterns, this new one won't give you much trouble. It's another common strum that's just a slight variation on the others you've learned (**Figure 8–5**).

You can listen to an MP3 file of this strumming pattern on my About.com site: http://about.com/guitar/audiostrum5. Take some time to get the rhythm locked in your head. Say "down-up-down-up up-down" along with the audio clip. The sample is long enough to play along with, too, so try playing along with it using a G major chord. Once you get familiar with it, listen to the other MP3 file of the strum at a faster speed (http://about.com/guitar/audiostrum5fast), and try playing along with that.

We'll use our same basic strumming technique. Keep the up-and-down strumming motion going on the 1-and-2-and-3-and-4-and count, using downstrokes on the numbers, and upstrokes on the *and*s. When you get to the fifth and eighth strums in the pattern, which occur on the 3-count and the *and* of the 4-count, just lift the pick away from the strings and "miss" them with their strums. Then lower the pick again so you're on the strings with the next strum.

Things to remember:

- Make sure to strum directly over the sound hole.
- Make sure all the strings are ringing clearly.
- Make sure the volume of your downstrokes and upstrokes are equal.
- Be careful not to strum too hard, as this often causes strings to buzz or rattle.
- Be careful not to strum too softly either, as this will produce a "wimpy" sound. Your pick should be striking the strings with a relatively firm, even stroke.
- Think of your elbow as being the top of a pendulum; your arm should swing up and down from it in a steady motion, never pausing at any time.
- Though your arm provides the swing, the bulk of the picking motion should come from a rotation of the wrist, rather than from the forearm. Do not keep your wrist stiff.
- The key to learning strumming patterns is to be able to "hear" the pattern in your head before you try to play it.

Figure 8–5   Strumming pattern #5

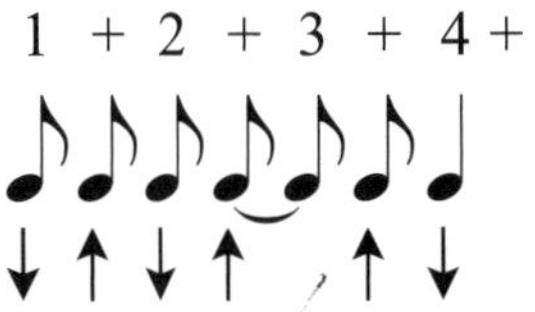

Now let's put these new chords and strumming patterns to use by learning some new songs.

Songs You Can Play Now

Here are three songs you can try that incorporate strumming techniques you've learned.

○ "Best of My Love," *the Eagles*
www.geocities.com/etheltheaardvark/bestofmylove.txt

○ "Hotel California," *the Eagles*
www.chordie.com/chord.pere/www.rockmagic.net/guitar-tabs/
eagles/hotel_california.crd

○ "Yer So Bad," *Tom Petty & the Heartbreakers*
www.chordie.com/chord.pere/www.ultimate-guitar.com/print.
php?what=tab&id=5692

I hope that by now you look forward to your half hour of daily practice time. For most guitarists it's one of the best parts of the day, and the half hour seems to fly by once they pick up the instrument.

Don't spend all of your time trying to play barre chords— chances are you'll just end up frustrated and with very sore fingers. If you want to conquer barre chords, however, you'll have to put in a few minutes' worth of work on them every time you pick up your guitar.

Here's how to spend your daily practice time:

1. Make sure your guitar is in tune.
2. Warm up by playing the new 2-octave chromatic scale slowly and accurately. Try not to hesitate when switching

▶▶▶
Try the new strumming pattern that you learned in this chapter on the Eagles song "Best of My Love." Strum the Tom Petty song "Yer So Bad" using the down, down-up, up-down-up pattern that you learned in Chapter 5.

strings. Once you know it beginning on the fifth fret of the sixth string, try starting it farther up the fingerboard.

3. Review the new seventh chords, plus your open chords, power chords, the B minor barre chord, and the F major and F minor barre chords. You've learned a lot, so it's important to keep all these chords organized in your mind.

4. Review all five strumming patterns we've covered. Try switching from chord to chord while using these patterns.

5. Try to play all of the songs listed in this chapter, and also keep playing those from previous chapters. Try committing one or several songs to memory. Pick an easy one to start with.

As we continue to learn more and more material, it becomes easy to overlook the techniques learned in earlier chapters. They are all still important, so it is advisable to keep going over previous chapters to be sure you're not forgetting anything.

Also, remember to force yourself to practice the things you are weakest at doing. Turn those into your strongest techniques.

ELSEWHERE ON THE WEB

▶ The guitarist Richie Havens was introduced to millions through the original Woodstock music festival in 1969, where he gave an inspired and heartfelt performance that featured his unique style on the acoustic guitar. One interesting aspect of Havens' guitar style is the prominent role played by the thumb on his fretting hand. On his Web site Havens shares his thumb-heavy guitar technique using open D tuning. Just go to www.richie havens.com/HM3365.htm.

Get Linked

*You can find more information on the subjects we've discussed in this chapter on my **About.com** site. Check out these helpful links.*

LEARNING TO LOVE JAZZ

An explanation of how to listen to jazz, as well as some great jazz radio stations and suggested CDs

 http://about.com/guitar/lovejazz

GUITAR TAB SOFTWARE

Links to useful software that makes it easier to create and read tablature

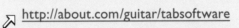 http://about.com/guitar/tabsoftware

Chapter 9

Fingerpicking

More Barre Chords

I hope you're having fun with your newfound ability to play major and minor chords all up and down the fingerboard—in any key you like—thanks to the power of barre chords to unlock the potential of the whole neck. There are four essential barre chord shapes. In Chapter 8 you learned three of them: the major barre with the root on the sixth string, the minor barre with the root on the sixth string, and the minor barre with the root on the fifth string. It's worth our time to take another look at those chord shapes now (see **Figure 9–1** on the following page).

Knowing the names of the notes on the sixth and fifth strings is essential to using your barre chords well. If someone asks you to play a D minor chord, not only can you do that now with the barre chords you know; you also have your choice of two different **voicings** of the barre chord to offer, if you remember that D falls on the tenth fret of the sixth string and on the fifth fret of the fifth string. Let's try that now. First play your minor barre with the root on the

Figure 9–1   Layout of three diagrams of barre chords

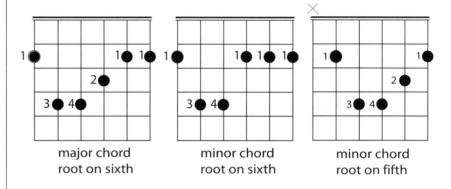

major chord
root on sixth

minor chord
root on sixth

minor chord
root on fifth

ASK YOUR GUIDE

The stretch between the first and second fingers feels weird. How can I make it easier?

▶ This hand stretch feels unnatural in the beginning, but there are ways to make it easier. You can use the neck of your instrument to help. Try grasping the neck near the headstock with your thumb and first finger over the top of the neck, and your second, third, and fourth fingers below the neck. With the neck held between your first and second fingers like this, you can gently force the stretch a little every day until it feels more natural.

sixth string using the D (tenth fret) as the root. Now try your minor barre with the root on the fifth string using the D (fifth fret) as the root. Hear how they're the same chord? And if you continue down the fingerboard to open position and play your D minor chord, you get yet another descending voicing of the chord. All three voicings use the same notes, but stack them in a different order.

Now let's learn the last of the essential barre chord shapes, the major barre with the root on the fifth string.

We've left this chord shape until last. It's the trickiest of the four to play, because it calls for new fretting-hand positions.

There are three commonly used fingerings for the fifth-string major barre chord. The first involves using your first finger to barre strings five through one (the sixth string has an X above it), while the second, third, and fourth fingers play the remaining notes as indicated in **Figure 9–2**. This is probably the best way to accurately play the chord, ensuring that each string rings clearly.

You'll notice that this chord shape requires a new kind of stretch in which the first finger reaches out toward the headstock to get in position. This particular hand stretch is one that will be called for more and more as you advance on guitar, both for playing chords and for scales, so it's good to become familiar with it.

One common alternate fingering for this chord is to use the third finger to barre all the necessary notes on the fourth, third, and second strings. The problem many people have with this fingering is the difficulty in getting the third finger to NOT fret the note on the first string. A common solution is to omit the note on the first string, since that note already exists elsewhere in the chord.

The other alternate fingering for this chord is to use your fourth finger to barre all the necessary notes on the fourth, third, and second strings. Some people prefer this fingering because the smaller size of the fourth finger makes it easier to clear the first string so that it rings clearly, and also because it's an easier stretch between the first-finger barre and the fourth-finger barre.

Practice playing the chord using all three fingerings. It will certainly be difficult at first, but, like all the things we're studying, it will get easier with time. Play each fingering of the chord one string at a time, to be certain all notes are ringing clearly.

With these four most essential barre chords, you can play literally thousands of songs. You should be able to replicate all of the open chord songs you've learned (provided they contain only major and minor chords) using barre chords. Memorizing the notes on the sixth and fifth strings and getting the chords to ring clearly will take time, but if you practice them every day, you can minimize that time. Try to devote a little time to playing your barre chords each time you pick up the guitar. Things to try:

- Learn all four barre chords well. Remember the shape, the type (major or minor), and which string the root is on.
- Call out a random chord (say E♭ major). Now, see how quickly you can play it on the sixth and the fifth strings.

Figure 9–2   Fifth string major barre chord

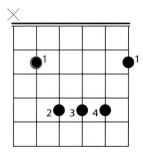

- notes on the fourth, third, and second strings can also be played with 3rd finger

- note on the first string is optional

- When playing songs, try moving to the closest voicing for the next chord. For example, when changing from G major to C major, instead of sliding the major barre with root on sixth from the third fret up to the eighth fret, try switching to the C major with root on fifth. Both of their roots are right there on the third fret.

Introduction to Fingerpicking

Up until now we've only used a pick to **pluck** the strings of the guitar. Now we'll put our picks down and explore another universe of picking-hand technique—**fingerpicking**.

Fingerpicking uses the thumb and the first three fingers (sometimes the fourth one gets into the act, too) of the picking hand to pluck the strings individually, either all at once or in arpeggiated rhythms, which means the strings are plucked in rhythmic sequences.

Fingerpicking also allows you to play **polyrhythms**, which means playing two different rhythms at the same time that interact with each other. You can make your guitar sound like two people are playing at once with this technique.

We'll begin with some simple rhythms and work our way up to the tricky stuff.

First you have to get your picking hand in the correct position. Start by centering the palm of your picking hand over the sound hole of the guitar.

Curl your fingers and thumb at your second knuckle, and turn your hand so that your fingertips rest underneath the strings (so your second knuckles point toward the floor). See **Figure 9–3**.

Your hand should be in a loose claw shape. See **Figure 9–4**.

We'll start by playing a D major chord, so we'll only be playing the bottom four strings. Poise your thumb on the upper side of the fourth string. Your first finger will rest underneath the third string. Your second finger will rest underneath the second string. Finally,

Figure 9–3   Front view of fingerpicking hand

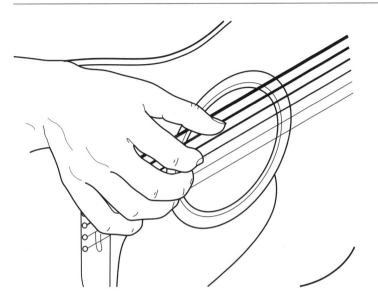

Figure 9–4   Side view of fingerpicking hand

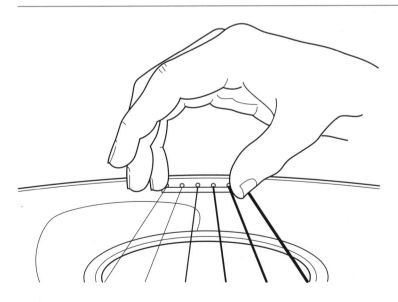

ELSEWHERE ON THE WEB

▶ Want to hear some examples of the best fingerpickers on guitar? Sites such as Amazon.com and TowerRecords.com offer a very convenient way to check out the albums of any fingerpicking master you like (or any other albums for that matter). Do a search for the musician you're interested in, pick an album that he or she recorded, and scroll down the page. The sites will let you sample a short portion of every track on the album free! Here are some names to start with: John Fahey, Joni Mitchell, Leo Kottke, Michael Hedges, and Alex DeGrassi.

your third finger will rest underneath the first string. Let your fingers settle in this position, trying to make them feel as comfortable as possible. Then allow your fourth finger to drop naturally until it rests on the top of the guitar. This finger will remain resting on the guitar top and will **anchor** your hand, meaning it will keep the rest of your hand in a stable position relative to the instrument. Note that the fourth finger anchor is not shown in **Figure 9–5**.

Form an open position D major chord with your fretting hand. Now, using a downward motion with the inside edge of your thumb, play the open note on the fourth string. Your thumbnail should make contact with the string. As it releases the string, the pluck occurs. Your thumb should not move far; return it to its original position after you play the note. Try this several times, until the motion feels comfortable and natural.

Then, play the third string, using an upward motion with the tip of your first finger. The slight contact of your fingernail against the

Figure 9–5   Top view of fingerpicking hand

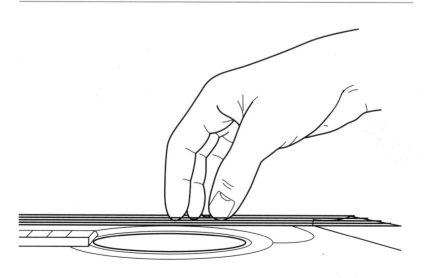

string will create the pluck. Again, there should be minimal movement by the finger, and you should return it to its original position after playing the note. Examine the motion closely as you do it, and repeat it until it feels natural. Repeat this process with your second finger on the second string, and finally with your third finger on the first string. Your fingers should always remain curled, and the motion should come primarily from the second knuckle down.

Now, try playing the strings with one pluck each, in order from the fourth string to first. Be sure to use the correct fingers in your picking hand, and watch for any problems that might be hanging you up. You can listen to an MP3 file of this fingerpicking pattern on my About.com site: http://about.com/guitar/audiofingerpickd.

In terms of changing chords the general concept of simple fingerpicking is this: The thumb moves to play the bass strings when the chord changes, while the three remaining fingers remain stationary, each responsible for playing its own string. Let's use this concept as we play the following example (see **Figure 9–6**).

This chord change introduces us to a new chord, the **69 chord**, in this case the C^{69} (pronounced "C six nine"). The name of this

Figure 9–6   D major and C^{69} chords

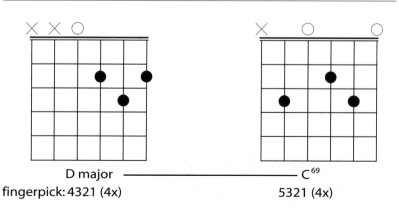

D major
fingerpick: 4321 (4x)

C^{69}
5321 (4x)

chord is based on the fact that it contains the 6th and 9th notes (A and D) of the C major scale.

All that's required to change from the D major to the C^{69} chord is to move your second finger from the second fret of the first string to the third fret of the fifth string. Give it a try. Nice sounding change, right?

Only one move in your fingerpicking hand will change—your thumb will move up to play the fifth string, instead of the fourth, on the C^{69}.

The pattern we'll play for the example in **Figure 9–6** is the fourth, third, second, and first strings four times on the D major, followed by the fifth, third, second, and first strings four times on the C^{69}. Repeat this pattern without stopping.

You can listen to an MP3 file of this fingerpicking pattern on my About.com site: http://about.com/guitar/audiofingerpickdtoc69.

Things to remember:

- Make sure your picking-hand fingers are curled at the second knuckle, as if they're grasping the strings. Never let your fingers straighten out.
- Your palm should move very little in the fingerpicking process. All the movement should be done with your fingers.
- Your fingers should move back into position as soon as they've plucked their note, so they're ready to pluck again.
- If the strings are ringing very quietly, it means you aren't plucking them hard enough.
- Just for your information: Some guitarists choose not to anchor the fourth finger on the bridge of the guitar when they fingerpick, instead allowing the picking hand to float freely above the instrument. Both methods have merit, but I suggest you anchor your fourth finger while you're

starting out because it ensures that your fingers will remain in a consistent position relative to the guitar.

Tricky Finger Moves

Now that we've explored a whole new way to use the picking hand with fingerpicking, let's look at some different ways to use the fretting hand as well, beginning with ways to create notes using just the fretting hand. These techniques will give your fingers a new kind of dexterity and allow you to play scales and musical phrases faster than if you had to pick every note. What's more, if you combine these new fretting-hand moves with your fingerpicking, you'll be able to weave more intricate patterns of notes than ever before.

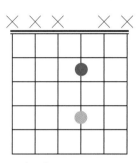

Figure 9–7   3rd string hammer-on

• play first note with first finger

• play second note with third finger

⬤ = first note

🔘 = second note

Let's begin with the hammer-on. Hammer-ons introduce a new technique for the fretting hand—generating a note without using your picking hand.

Until now, we've only played single notes in one way, which is by plucking the string with a pick or finger. While this is by far the most common method, there are alternate ways to play single notes. The hammer-on is one of them.

The concept of the hammer-on is fairly simple—you play a note and then, without plucking the string again, you play another note on a higher fret of the same string.

We'll try this hammer-on on the third string. Start by fretting the second fret of the third string with your first finger. Now, ready your third finger, poising it above the fourth fret of the third string, where it will come down in a moment (see **Figure 9–7**).

Use your pick to play the note on the second fret and then—without repicking the note—bring the tip of your third finger down firmly on the fourth fret and hold it down. If you do this with enough force, the note on the fourth fret should sound clearly, even though you don't repick it. If you didn't put your third finger on the string accurately enough, or with enough force, probably all that happened was that the first note stopped ringing. Try repeating the exercise until the second note rings out clearly.

You can listen to an MP3 file of this hammer-on, played at three different speeds, on my About.com site: http://about.com/guitar/audiohammeron.

- If you can't get the second note to ring, be sure you're putting your fingertip down directly on the string. If you're not accurate, you won't get good results.
- Try repeating this technique on different strings, and on different frets.
- Hammer two fingers onto a string. For example, start at the fifth fret, then hammer onto the sixth fret, then the seventh.

Now let's move on to pull-offs. Pull-offs illustrate a second way to generate a note without using your picking hand. The pull-off is a guitar technique that is, in a way, the exact opposite of a hammer-on. You'll start executing the pull-off technique by putting your third and first fingers on the fourth and second frets of the third string, as illustrated in **Figure 9–8**. Play the string with your pick, and let the note that you're playing with your third finger sound. Then remove your third finger from the string. As you do this, make a slight downward tugging motion against the string with your third finger. This tug should cause the note that your first finger is fretting to ring out. The first few times you try it, the string may stop ringing as you remove your finger. Keep practicing this technique, and you'll get it (see **Figure 9–8**).

You can listen to an MP3 file of this pull-off, played at three different speeds, on my About.com site: http://about.com/guitar/audiopulloff.

Figure 9–8   3rd string pull-off

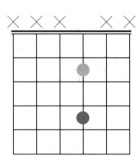

- play first note with third finger
- play second note with first finger

● = first note
● = second note

Once you start getting the hang of these techniques it's important to challenge yourself a little more, by trying to play things that combine multiple hammer-ons and pull-offs in a row. One of the best ways to do this is to try playing scales—ascending with hammer-ons, and descending with pull-offs.

You can listen to an MP3 file of the blues scale, played using hammer-ons ascending and using pull-offs descending, on my About.com site: http://about.com/guitar/audiobshammerpull.

Things to try:

- Hammering onto a note, then pulling off to the original note. Repeat this as long as possible, without repicking the string.
- Play all the other scales we've learned, using hammer-on and pull-off techniques.
- Try including hammer-ons and pull-offs whenever you play guitar. Most songs that include single notes use these techniques.
- Remember—use your fingertips on the frets instead of the pads of your fingers.

Open Tunings in C

In Chapter 8 you learned four of the most common and popular open tunings. Now we'll look at two alternate tunings in the key of C that are slightly more obscure but that also open up new chord possibilities to add to your repertoire.

Let's begin with **Open C tuning**, which changes the strings to C G C G C E.

To get into Open C tuning, start by tuning your sixth string down two whole steps to C.

Then tune your fifth string down a whole step to G. Check the tuning with the third (G) string. Next, tune your fourth string down a tone to C. Check the tuning with the sixth (C) string.

WHAT'S HOT

▶ If you want to hear a guitarist who has made a career out of using hammer-ons and pull-offs, check out the music of Stanley Jordan. This innovative player approaches the guitar more like a piano, using both of his hands on the fingerboard to play separate chord and melodic parts by using hammer-ons and pull-offs almost exclusively. Start with his 1985 breakthrough album, *Magic Touch*. Although Jordan uses an electric guitar on this album, he also uses the same technique on acoustic guitar.

Finally, tune your second string up a half step to C. Check the tuning with the fourth (C) string.

You can listen to a sound file of this Open C tuning on my About. com site. Just go to http://about.com/guitar/audioopenctuning.

In this tuning the guitar is tuned to a C major chord, and utilizes a very low sixth string to give the guitar a big, full sound.

Check out this Ben Harper tune "Breakin' Down" that's played in open C using a slide. You can try using your finger for simplicity's sake, however. You only need one finger across one fret to play this entire song. Just go to http://flarere.free.fr/Autres/Benharper/breakin_down.txt.

Now let's move on to **Low C tuning**, which changes the strings to C G D G A D.

To get into Low C tunings, start by tuning your sixth string down two whole steps to C.

Then tune your fifth string down a tone to G. Check the tuning with the third (G) string.

Next, tune your second string down a tone to A. Check with the second fret of your third string. Finally, tune your first string down a tone to D. Check with the open fourth string (D).

You can listen to a sound file of this Low C tuning on my About. com site. Just go to http://about.com/guitar/audiolowctuning.

Another somewhat unusual tuning, low C tuning, is most often used in Celtic music. You can create some unique sounds with this tuning.

You're probably familiar with the classic Irish song "Danny Boy." Here's a transcription of guitarist El McMeen's arrangement of this famous song, written for a guitar in low C tuning: www.elmcmeen .com/transcriptions/Danny%20Boy.PDF.

Nashville Tuning

All of the open tunings we've explored up to now have merely required retuning the existing strings on the guitar to notes other than the standard E A D G B E. The **Nashville tuning** puts a new twist on this process—the notes of the strings stay the same but the tuning requires changing the type of strings your instrument normally uses.

You may recall that on a 12-string guitar the sixth, fifth, fourth and third string pairs have one string tuned to normal pitch and the other string tuned one octave higher. The Nashville tuning is accomplished by replacing the lowest four strings on your guitar with the high-octave strings from a set of 12-string strings—thus the process is also referred to as "high-stringing" your guitar. The result is that the span of notes covered by the open strings is only two octaves instead of the normal three and the open strings reach their highest pitch on the fourth (G) string.

The sound produced by the Nashville tuning is narrower and more homogenous than normal, and the notes being closer together gives the sound a shimmering effect similar to the sound produced by a 12-string guitar.

You can hear the Nashville tuning used on the song "Hey You" from the *Pulse* album by Pink Floyd (Columbia 1995). If you don't have that album, look it up on Amazon.com where you can listen to a sample—the whole sample prominently features the guitar in Nashville tuning.

We've looked at seven alternate tunings now, which makes for a good introduction to the subject. There are many more open tunings out there to explore, each one of which is worth a try to see if it appeals to your ear and your imagination.

TOOLS YOU NEED

▶ D'Addario makes a couple of sets of strings made especially for Nashville tuning where they give you the octave strings for the sixth through third strings and normal strings for the second and first strings. This will save you from having to buy a whole set of 12-string strings just to get the six you need for this tuning. The normal gauge set for acoustic guitar is the D'Addario EJ38H High Strung / Nashville Tuning set, and there's a light gauge set made for electric guitar called D'Addario EXL150H Nashville High Strung Electric Guitar which can also be used on acoustic guitar for a lighter feel. You can find the acoustic set here: www.stringsand beyond.com/dejhisttuphb.html.

Songs You Can Play Now

Try out your fingerpicking on "Everybody Hurts"—it's a simple pattern and it's all written out for you in tab. The **chord progression** in "Layla" includes a couple of barre chords. On "Day Tripper," play the third and last notes of the famous intro phrase using hammer-ons. And on "Free Falling," try using all barre chords to play the song in addition to playing it in open position.

- "Everybody Hurts," *by R.E.M.*
  www.olga.net/archive/main/r/rem/everybody_hurts.crd?printer=0

- "Layla," *(acoustic) by Eric Clapton*
  www.chordie.com/chord.pere/www.ultimate-guitar.com/print.php?what=tab&id=63657

- "Day Tripper," *the Beatles*
  www.chordie.com/chord.pere/flarere.free.fr/Autres/Beatles/14/Daytripper.txt

- "Free Falling," *Tom Petty*
  www.chordie.com/chord.pere/www.ultimate-guitar.com/print.php?what=tab&id=5655

Hopefully you've gotten into the routine of picking up your guitar every day to practice. If not, don't give up—just try to pick it up one more day this week than you did last week.

Here are some things you'll want to focus on:

1. Make sure your guitar is in tune.
2. Warm up by playing a blues scale, making sure you're using alternate picking. Then, see if you can play it using hammer-ons and pull-offs.

▶▶▶

Now you can learn music that requires fingerpicking, hammer-ons/pull-offs, barre chords, and more.

3. Review the new major barre with root on the fifth string, plus the other three barre chords we've learned so far.

4. Review all strumming patterns we've covered. You've learned five strumming patterns now—the basic strum and four variations. Try switching from chord to chord while using these patterns.

5. Spend some time playing fingerpicked songs. Practice moving from chord to chord randomly, using a steady fingerpicking pattern.

6. Practice your hammer-ons and pull-offs for a minute or two.

7. Try to play all of the songs listed in this chapter, and also keep playing those from previous chapters.

If you're feeling confident with everything we've learned so far, try to find a few songs you're interested in, and learn them on your own. You can go to either the easy song tabs archive (http://about .com/guitar/easysongtabs) or the guitar tab area of my Web site (http://about.com/guitar/tabchordslyrics) to hunt down the music that you're the most inspired by. Try memorizing some of these songs, rather than always looking at the music to play them.

Get Linked

*You can find more information on the subjects we've discussed in this chapter on my **About.com** site. Check out this helpful link.*

HARMONIC MINOR SCALE

Here's a lesson in using the exotic sounding harmonic minor scale. Once you learn it, try playing it using your new hammer-ons and pull-offs.

 http://about.com/guitar/harmonicminorscale

Chapter 10

Advancing Both Hands

More Advanced Fingerpicking

As you spend more time fingerpicking, you'll appreciate the delicate complexity this technique adds to your guitar playing. In this chapter we'll expand on the fingerpicking concepts you learned in Chapter 9 and learn how to apply them to chord changes.

Remember that keeping your picking-hand fingers curled is extremely important. If your fingers are even somewhat straight when fingerpicking, you need to adjust your technique. Your palm should move very little in the fingerpicking process. All the movement should be done with your fingers.

When you're playing the exercise tabbed in **Figure 10–1** (see following page), it is important to hold down the chord shape with your fretting hand. Each bar in this tab has four beats. For the first bar, hold down the D major chord (xx0232) for the entire four beats. In the second bar, move to the C^{add9} (x30030) for the first two beats, and then to the G^6/B (x20030) for the last two beats. Repeat this pattern without stopping.

Figure 10-1   New fingerpicking pattern #1

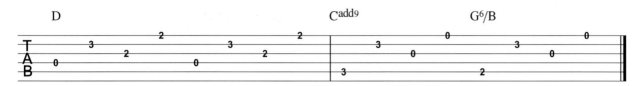

Finger the new chord C^{add9}, which is a C major chord with the ninth note of the scale, D, added, using your second finger on the fifth string and your third finger on the second string. Finger the new chord G^6/B, which is a G major chord with the sixth note of the scale, E, added and a B in the bass, using your first finger on the fifth string, leaving your third finger in the same position on the second string. Note that for all three chords in this progression your third finger remains in exactly the same place and never has to lift off the fingerboard.

The fingerpicking concept of the pattern in **Figure 10-1** is the same as in the previous lesson: Fingers one, two, and three play the top three strings, while the thumb "floats" to play notes on the fourth and fifth strings. The picking pattern has changed somewhat, though—we're no longer playing the strings in order. Play this exercise slowly, making sure that your hand position is good and that you're always using the correct finger to play the correct string.

Figure 10-2   New fingerpicking pattern #2

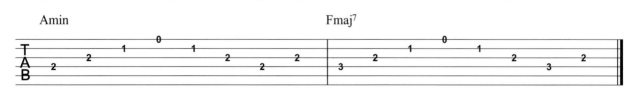

The **ABOUT.com** *Guide to* **Acoustic Guitar**

You can listen to an MP3 file of this new fingerpicking pattern #1 on my About.com site: http://about.com/guitar/audiofinger pick1.

Now look at **Figure 10–2**. This one should be pretty easy—your thumb plays all of its notes on the fourth string, and the only thing that changes from the A minor chord (xx2210) to the F major 7 chord (xx3210) is that the note on the fourth string moves up one fret.

Each bar in this tab has four beats. For the first bar, hold down the A minor chord for the entire four beats. In the second bar, hold down the F major 7 for the entire four beats. Repeat this pattern without stopping.

To make switching chords as easy as possible, fret the A minor chord so your third finger is on the fourth string, your second finger is on the third string (on the same fret), and your first finger is on the second string. Then you just have to slide your third finger up one fret to play the F major 7, and back down to return to the A minor. Again, practice this pattern slowly at first.

You can listen to an MP3 file of this new fingerpicking pattern #2 on my About.com site: http://about.com/guitar/audiofinger pick2.

Leading Bass and Alternate Bass Strumming

Up until now we've always played the exact same strings with each strum in the strumming patterns you've learned. In this chapter we'll explore two ways of playing single notes combined with a full strum.

Check out **Figure 10–3**. This simple G major strum uses a strumming rhythm we've studied before: down, down-up, up-down-up. The only difference is that now, on the first strum of the pattern, we're only hitting the sixth string. This is a **leading bass strum**, meaning that a single bass note leads into the strumming that follows for the rest of the pattern.

TOOLS YOU NEED

▶ It's time for an introduction to another common form of guitar shorthand. When you see six characters inside parentheses, like this—(xx0232)—you're being told what to do with each of the six strings in tab language. In this example, you're being told by the first two Xs not to strum the sixth and fifth string. The 0 means to play the open fourth string, and the 232 means to fret the third, second, and first strings on the second, third, and second frets. Look familiar? It's a D major chord.

When playing this single note, it's important to keep the same strumming motion that you use when playing a full chord. Your pick should still pass across all six strings, but should only play the sixth. You can accomplish this by slightly pulling the pick away from the strings after you've struck the sixth string on the first strum. Practice this technique—you'll find it gets easier and easier as you go along.

Figure 10–3   Simple G major strum

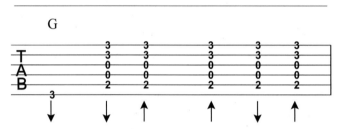

You can listen to an MP3 file of this simple G major strum on my About.com site: http://about.com/guitar/audiogmajorstrum.

The C/G **alternate bass note strum** is a pattern you commonly find in old folk songs, traditional country and western, polka music, and in some other styles. You might find this strum a little bit tricky to play accurately at first, but soon you'll be able to play it with ease.

Play the chord shown in **Figure 10–4** by first fretting a C major chord. Then move your third finger to the third fret of the sixth string, and put your fourth finger on the third fret of the fifth string. Hold this shape throughout the pattern.

The strumming pattern for this tablature is a simple one: down, down-up, down, down-up. As in the previous strum, we will be playing some single notes, followed by full chord strums. The main difference with this strum is that now we're alternating between two bass notes.

Strike the fifth string with a down strum, then strum the full chord: down-up. Now, play the sixth string with a down strum; then again play the full chord with a down-up strumming pattern. This, of course, will get easier with practice (see **Figure 10–4**).

Figure 10–4   C/G alternate strum

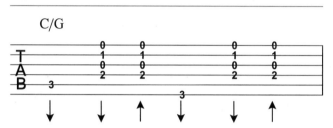

You can listen to an MP3 file of this C/G alternate strum on my About.com site: http://about.com/guitar/audiocgaltstrum.

Here are some things to remember:

- When playing these patterns, it is extremely important to keep your strumming motion constant, whether you're playing the single notes or the full chords. You might find that at first you accidentally play several strings when trying to strum one string. Don't let this get to you; just try to remedy the problem.
- Be sure to master these new strums, because we'll get into much more complex variations of them in future lessons.

Introduction to Slash Chords

The chord example in the last strumming pattern uses a C/G (referred to as "C over G") chord. This is just one of the hundreds of these types of chords that you'll find in popular music. They're referred to as **slash chords**.

ASK YOUR GUIDE

Should I be doing anything special to my fingernails for guitar playing?

▶ If you're serious about wanting to fingerpick well, you should consider growing the nails on your picking hand slightly. The contact of your fingernail against the string creates a clean pluck and gives you a "brighter" sound than if you pick the string with just your fingertip. The fingernails on your fretting hand should always be cut short, so that they do not stick out any farther than your fingertip. This is because you always want to fret strings with the very tips of your fingers.

Reading these chords is simple. The letter to the left of the slash is the type of chord—in this case, a C major chord. The note to the right of the slash is the bass note in the chord—a G in this circumstance. So, a C/G chord is a C major chord with the note G in the bass. If you look at the chord in the alternate bass strumming pattern we just studied, you can clearly see the C major chord, with the G on the third fret of the sixth string also being fretted in the bass.

The following sections describe a few common slash chords.

D/F♯ ("D over F♯") is a standard D major chord with an F♯ in the bass. Playing the D over F♯ brings us to a new technique—using the thumb to fret notes. That's right, the thumb is not always confined to the back of the guitar neck. At times it can leap over the top of the neck and join the fingers in forming a chord, and this is one of those times. Play this chord using the normal fingering for an open D major, and then wrap the thumb over the top of the neck of the guitar and use it to fret the second fret of the sixth string (the F♯).

A/C♯ ("A over C♯") is an A major chord with a C♯ in the bass. It is usually played by barring the second fret of the fourth, third, and second strings with your first finger, and playing the fourth fret of the fifth string (the C♯) with either the third finger or the fourth finger.

C/E ("C over E") is a C major chord with an E in the bass. It is usually played by simply fretting an open C major chord, and then including the open low E string in the strum.

A minor/G ("A minor over G") is an A minor chord with a G in the bass. This is usually played by fretting an open A minor chord, and then using the fourth finger to play the third fret of the sixth string (the G).

Looking for some new things to try? The following two exercises are designed to help you make up your own exercises to practice as you go along. Playing little games with the material and techniques you're learning, such as making up your own slash chords or chord progressions, is one of the best ways to figure out the path on guitar that most interests you. I encourage you to try your own variations of any exercise you might be working on. Ultimately, this will lead to developing your own unique guitar style.

- Invent your own slash chords by thinking of a chord type, then picking a random note to play in the bass. Next, try to figure out how to play these chords. They won't all sound wonderful, but you may stumble upon some that you like. And this is great practice for learning the names of notes on the fingerboard.
- Try making up some chord progressions that use the slash chords explained in this chapter, or other slash chords. Here are a few to get you started:
  - A minor–A minor/G–F major
  - G major–D/F#–E minor
  - D minor–D minor/C–G/B–C major

More Tricky Finger Moves

Here are two more fretting-hand techniques that will allow you to generate notes on the guitar without having to pluck them with your pick. The **slide** gives you the ability to create a chromatic scale between the first and last notes you're sliding between with just one finger of your fretting hand. When you slide slowly you get a lot of definition between those chromatic notes; sliding fast creates more of a textural effect. **String bending** lets you generate new notes by stretching the string with your finger. You'll probably recognize this sound when you try it, because it's one of the signature sounds of the guitar.

Figure 10–5 Slide #1

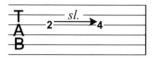

The slide is a popular guitar technique. All budding guitar players should master it. Learning to slide well will take practice, but you should get the hang of the technique almost immediately.

The concept is to fret a note and play it, and then slide your finger to another note on the same string and hold it, without re-picking. Start on the third string, second fret. Play that note, and then briskly slide your finger up to the fourth fret on the same string and hold the note. Give it a try (see **Figure 10–5**).

If you're like most people who try this for the first time, the note probably died as soon as you started to slide it. The key is to keep exerting downward pressure on the string with your finger while sliding the note. Try it again, making sure you keep pressing down the notes as you slide.

You can listen to an MP3 file of slide #1, played at three different speeds, on my About.com site: http://about.com/guitar/audioslide1.

This second slide is almost the same as the first—it just adds another step. This time, slide on the third string from the second fret to the fourth fret, then back to the second fret, all without re-picking the string (see **Figure 10–6**).

Figure 10–6 Slide #2

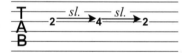

You can listen to an MP3 file of slide #2, played at two different speeds, on my About.com site: http://about.com/guitar/audio slide2.

Try to use each of the guitar techniques we study to play many different things. For example, try playing the A blues scale using the sliding technique, picking each string only once and then sliding to the other notes on that string. To play it this way, you'll need to use only one finger to play the entire scale.

You can listen to an MP3 file of the A blues scale played with slides on my About.com site: http://about.com/guitar/audioslide3.

You can try something similar using your hammer-ons and pull-offs to play the different scales you've learned.

Here are some things you should know:

- It's normal to hear a squeaking sound when you're sliding on the lower strings. That's because of the ridges on the winding that wraps around those strings. You'll notice that this doesn't happen as much on the thinner unwound strings.
- When sliding, press your finger down only as hard as you need to in order for the note to keep ringing. Pressing too hard will slow your finger down, and the slide won't sound smooth.
- When sliding to another fret, focus your eyes on the fret you're about to slide to. Your finger will naturally slide to that fret.

String bending creates one of the guitar's most distinctive sounds. This bending technique is used when playing single-note riffs and solos to give the guitar a more "vocal" quality. It's done by stretching the string while holding a note down to raise the pitch of that note. Although it's a technique used mostly by lead guitar players, even three-chord folk guitarists will find uses for string bends from time to time.

You've learned some interesting new techniques in the past few chapters, but none that will give you as much trouble in the beginning as this one. Bending the strings far enough to get the pitch to change takes a good deal of effort, especially at first. But as you play more, your fretting hand will become stronger, and bending will become easier and more natural.

Some guitarists use three fingers to **bend** the string, instead of just the finger on the fret they're trying to bend. You would accomplish this by first placing your third finger on the fret you're trying to bend. Place your first and second fingers on the two frets behind it, and exert pressure with all three fingers. This puts three times the

WHAT'S HOT

▶ One of the masters of the finger-sliding technique is the guitarist Robbie Robertson of The Band and many other groups. It's been said that when he first heard slide guitar on the radio he didn't know that it was played using a slide, so he tried to imitate the technique using just his fingers. This "misunderstanding" led to his developing his own unique approach to finger sliding, which became a key part of his guitar style.

Figure 10–7   String bend #1

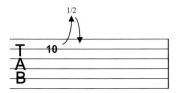

finger strength at your disposal and at the same time distributes the string pressure (read: pain) among all three fingers.

Let's look at the tab of our first exercise. Start by fretting the note on the tenth fret of the second string with your third finger. Your second finger should rest behind your third finger on the second string, ninth fret. Your first finger should rest behind your second finger on the second string, eighth fret (see **Figure 10–7**).

As indicated by the little arrow on the tab, our goal is to bend this note up a half step (also called a **semitone**), and then return the note to its original pitch. Play the tenth fret and then the eleventh fret, so you can hear the proper pitch of the note you're trying to bend up to. Then pick the note, and exert force in an upward motion (toward you), while still maintaining some pressure on the string so it keeps ringing, until you reach the upper note. Try to use all three fingers to bend the string in the beginning, not just the third finger. Then return the note to its original pitch.

Chances are that when you first attempt this, you won't get the pitch to change as much as you want. This is especially true because you're playing acoustic guitar, which is much harder to bend strings on than electric guitar. Most likely you haven't used these particular muscles before, and they'll take time to strengthen. Keep practicing, and you'll get the hang of it soon.

You can listen to an MP3 file of what string bend #1 should sound like on my About.com site: http://about.com/guitar/audio stringbend1.

Now let's step it up a notch.

This second exercise is exactly the same as the one in **Figure 10–7**, except this time the little arrow on the tab is telling us to bend the note up a whole step (also called a **tone** or **whole tone**).

Start by playing the tenth fret, and then the twelfth fret, to hear the pitch you're trying to bend the note up to. Now, while fretting the note on the tenth fret of the second string with your third finger, pick the note, bend it up until you reach the upper note, and then return it to its original pitch. Remember to use all three fingers in the beginning to help bend the note. Otherwise, you probably won't be able to push the note far enough (see **Figure 10–8**).

You can listen to an MP3 file of what string bend #2 should sound like on my About.com site: http://about.com/guitar/audio stringbend2.

Here are some things to remember:

- If the note is dying before you've completed the bend, you've probably stopped exerting enough pressure against the fingerboard to keep the note sounding. You should use all three fingers to do these bends in the beginning. Make sure you're pushing the strings in the direction of the sky, not the ground.
- Bends are almost always done on the top three strings, because they are lighter and easier to bend.
- It's easier to bend strings on the higher frets on the guitar. Down near the headstock, it gets very hard to bend.
- This is also the technique that puts the most string pressure on the still-developing calluses of your fretting hand. If you're practicing string bending and your fingers start to hurt, stop working on this technique for the day and come back to it tomorrow.
- It will take time to master this technique, so be patient.

Songs You Can Play Now

These songs use fingerpicking and/or strumming patterns that include single notes. For now, leave all the sevenths off the chords (for example, B minor 7 becomes B minor, and C major 7 becomes

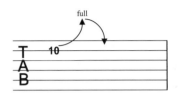

Figure 10–8   String bend #2

C major). There are a couple of slash chords—I'll let you figure out how to play them.

○ "The Weight," *The Band*
www.olga.net/archive/main/b/band/the_weight.crd

○ "More Than a Feeling," *Boston*
www.chordie.com/chord.pere/getsome.org/guitar/olga/chord-pro/b/Boston/MoreThanAFeeling.chopro

○ "Brian Wilson," *Barenaked Ladies*
www.geocities.com/SouthBeach/Sands/9129/brian%5Fwilson.html

○ "Is There Anybody Out There," *Pink Floyd*
www.guitarnoise.com/pink_floyd/the_wall/is_there_anybody_out_there_tab.txt

I can't emphasize enough the importance of going back over the previous chapters, to be sure you remember how to play everything we've studied. Here are some things you'll want to focus on:

1. Make sure your guitar is in tune.
2. Warm up by playing a blues scale, making sure you're using alternate picking.
3. See if you can play the blues scale using a slide technique.
4. Practice all barre chords we've covered, making sure you also review note names on the sixth and fifth strings. By this point, you should know these quite well. If not—review, review, review.
5. Play the new strumming patterns using a combination of single notes and chords. We'll be building on these in future chapters, so get them sounding perfect!

▶ ▶ ▶
When you play "The Weight," use the strumming pattern down, down, down, down-up. Play the A/G♯ chord with your first finger barring the notes on the second fret and your third finger fretting the fourth fret of the sixth string (4x222x). On the opening of "More Than a Feeling," your first three fingers remain by the first three strings, while your thumb "floats" to play the notes on the fourth, fifth, and sixth strings, similar to the first fingerpicking exercise we did in this chapter. And on "Brian Wilson," use the strumming pattern down, down-up, up-down-up.

6. Every time you pick up the guitar, play a few string bends. You'll get the hang of them in time.
7. Review slash chord theory, and make sure you understand it. Try playing a few slash chords that you make up yourself.
8. Try the fingerpicking patterns, and the two songs in this chapter's list that utilize fingerpicking.
9. Try to play all of the songs above, and also keep playing those from previous lessons.

Try to find a few songs you're interested in, and learn them on your own. You can use either the easy song tabs archive or the guitar tab area of my Web site to hunt down the music that you're the most inspired by. Try memorizing some of these songs, rather than always looking at the music to play them.

Get Linked

*You can find more information on my **About.com** site. Since the subject of this chapter is advancing both hands, you might enjoy challenging yourself to play some of the best-known guitar solos. Even though almost all of these solos are played on electric guitar, the picking and fingering challenges they present are just as applicable to acoustic guitar.*

100 GREATEST GUITAR SOLOS

Tablature of top-rated guitar solos in a *Guitar World* magazine readers' poll

 http://about.com/guitar/100solos

Chapter 11

Expanding Your Scales

More on 2-Octave Scales

Whether it was a lullabye or the "Doe, a deer" song, the major scale is most likely the first one you ever heard or were taught. The major scale is the foundation upon which our music system is built. It contains seven notes (do-re-mi-fa-so-la-ti). We're going to learn this scale on guitar, in two octaves.

This pattern for the major scale is a movable pattern, with the root on the sixth string. If you start the scale on the third fret of the sixth string, you're playing a G major scale. If you start at the eighth fret, you're playing a C major scale. Once you know this fingering pattern for the major scale, you can play it in any key you want.

It's extremely important when playing this scale to make sure your fretting hand stays in position. It should not move up or down the neck as you play.

Figure 11–1   Movable major scale

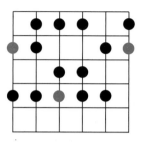

Figure 11–2   E Phrygian scale

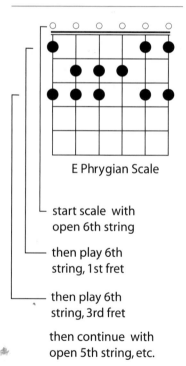

E Phrygian Scale

start scale with open 6th string

then play 6th string, 1st fret

then play 6th string, 3rd fret

then continue with open 5th string, etc.

Start the scale with your second finger on the sixth string (this is the root of the scale), followed by your fourth finger on the sixth string. Play the third note with your first finger on the fifth string, and so on. Each finger on your fretting hand is responsible for just one fret on the guitar when playing this scale. For example, when playing an A major scale (fifth fret), your first finger will play all notes on the fourth fret, your second finger will play all notes on the fifth fret, your third finger will play all notes on the sixth fret, and your fourth finger will play all notes on the seventh fret (see **Figure 11–1**).

You can hear this major scale played in the key of A (beginning on the fifth fret of the sixth string), first in a slowly ascending version, and then a faster version ascending and descending, on my About.com site: http://about.com/guitar/audioamajorscale.

Things to remember:

- As always, use alternate picking as your primary method of playing this scale. You can also practice the scale using all upstrokes, or all downstrokes.
- Memorize this scale. You'll use it extensively in years to come.
- Play the scale forward, then backward, in a slow, even tempo. Build up speed only when your technique at slower tempos is flawless. You don't want to practice your mistakes!

Introduction to Modes

The major scale is also the framework around which **modes** were created. The classical modes are a series of scales that grew out of ancient Greek music. They are centered around a C major scale, and each of the seven modes uses the same consecutive notes of that C major scale—but each mode begins on a different note of the scale. This means that in each mode the half steps and whole steps fall in different places, which is what gives each one its unique sound.

Each of the modes has a Greek name associated with it, said to derive from the area of ancient Greece where the mode was widely used. Here are the notes of the C major scale, and the mode associated with each note:

- C: Ionian
- D: Dorian
- E: Phrygian
- F: Lydian
- G: Mixolydian
- A: Aeolian
- B: Locrian

Because the guitar is designed around the key of E, we'll begin with the mode based on E, which is the Phrygian mode. We'll learn this scale in the open position (see **Figure 11–2**).

In this scale you will use your first finger to play all notes on the first fret of the guitar. Your second finger will play all notes on the second fret. Your third finger will play all notes on the third fret. Because there aren't any notes on the fourth fret in this scale, you won't need to use your fourth finger at all.

Start on the open sixth string and follow the diagram, playing each note indicated until you have reached the third fret on the first string.

To understand how each of the modes grows out of the same series of notes, let's look at what happens if we begin this exact same scale on a different note. We know that the modes are based on the notes of a C major scale—so if we start this scale on C we should have a major scale, right?

ELSEWHERE ON THE WEB

▶ If you'd like to learn more about the Greek modes and other types of modes, including how to use them, what emotions each one is known to convey, and some suggestions for further reading on the subject, check out this interesting report on Wikipedia. Just go to http://en.wikipedia.org/wiki/Musical_mode.

Figure 11–3   Basic Dorian
shape

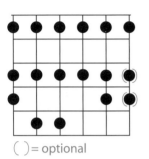

( ) = optional

Let's test this theory. Begin this scale on the C, which is the third fret of the fifth string, and play eight notes of the scale. Is it a major scale?

Things to remember:

- Use alternate picking throughout. Start the scale with a downstroke, and then start with an upstroke the next time.
- Once you've finished the scale, try playing it backward by starting at the first string, third fret, and playing all notes in exactly the reverse order of the original scale.
- The key here is accuracy, not speed! Start by playing the scale very slowly, making sure that each note is ringing clearly. When you can play a clean version with no mistakes, you can speed it up.

Introduction to the Dorian Mode

We've learned about modes, and the Phrygian mode in particular. Now let's spend some time exploring another mode, the Dorian, in greater depth.

Realistically speaking, becoming a great rock guitar soloist doesn't require an enormous amount of musical knowledge. Many good guitarists stick almost exclusively to pentatonic scales, blues scales, and assorted licks to create their solos. For the slightly more adventurous guitarist, however, there will be times when a pentatonic or blues scale just doesn't provide the right sound for the situation. This is where modes of the major scale, like the Phrygian and the Dorian modes, come into play.

The Dorian mode, when played as the two-octave pattern illustrated here, sounds like a minor scale (see **Figure 11–3**). Try playing it yourself, starting with your first finger on the sixth string.

Maintain your hand position throughout, stretching your fourth finger to play notes on the fourth and fifth frets of the pattern.

The root of this scale is the first note on the sixth string. For example, if you start the mode on the note A on the sixth string, you're playing an A Dorian mode.

You can listen to an MP3 file of the A Dorian mode on my About.com site: http://about.com/guitar/audioadorian.

Once you've got the hang of playing the Dorian mode across the neck, try playing it up and down a single string, as illustrated in **Figure 11–4**. Find the root of the scale on the string you're playing, then move up a whole step to the second note, up a half step to the third, up a whole step to the fourth, up a whole step to the fifth, up a whole step to the sixth, up a half step to the seventh, and up a whole step back to the root note again. Try picking one specific Dorian mode (for example, C Dorian) and playing it on all six strings, one string at a time.

The sound of the Dorian mode differs slightly from that of a natural minor scale. In a natural minor scale (or what might be referred to as a regular minor scale), the sixth note of the scale is flatted. In the Dorian mode, this sixth note is not flatted. What results is a scale that can sound a little more "bright," or some might say even slightly "jarring" to the ear (note—this can be good if it's what you're going for). In popular music, the Dorian mode works exceptionally well in minor chord **vamps** (situations where the music lingers on one minor chord for a long amount of time). If a song is stuck on an A minor chord for a long time, a guitarist might try playing an A Dorian mode over that part of the song to introduce some new color into the sound.

Examples of the Dorian Mode Now that you've had an introduction to the Dorian mode, it's time to check out a few examples

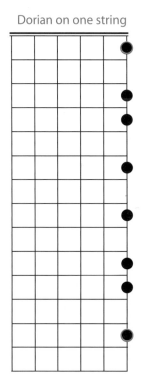

Figure 11–4   Dorian scale on one string

Dorian on one string

on my About.com site. Go to http://about.com/guitar/dorianlicks. This link will bring you to just a few examples of the many great solo-ists who use the Dorian mode in their improvisation. Try listening to and playing through each example, and let your mind absorb the sound the Dorian mode creates.

The first example you'll find when you go to the site is a solo from Carlos Santana's song "Evil Ways." Santana has long been one of the guitarists experimenting with the sounds of the Dorian mode, among other scales. The Dorian mode has more notes than simple pentatonic scales, which gives Santana more notes to explore. The guitar tablature excerpt on my About.com site finds Santana soloing over a G minor to C chord progression using the G Dorian mode. As is customary for him, however, Santana throws in bits of the blues scale and other scales within this same solo.

Want to hear how the solo sounds? You can listen to an MP3 file of this solo on my About.com site: http://about.com/guitar/audio evilways.

Tony Iommi, guitarist for Black Sabbath, is another guitarist noted for using the Dorian mode in his guitar solos. Iommi plays notes from the E Dorian mode over the static E minor chord in "Planet Caravan." The Dorian sound really helps to create a dis-tinct mood in this situation. Iommi doesn't just stick to Dorian, however—the guitarist also uses notes from the E blues scale, among others, to vary the sound of his solo.

When learning to play the guitar—or any instrument—listen-ing can sometimes be as helpful to your progress as playing the music yourself. You can listen to an MP3 file of this solo on my About.com site: http://about.com/guitar/audioplanetcaravan.

The third piece of tablature on the site is a great example of the Dorian mode used as the basis for a song riff. "Loud Love" by

Soundgarden is based on the E Dorian mode, played up and down the sixth and fifth strings. The fourth fret on the fifth string (Db) is the note that really tips the ear off to the sound of the mode. Try playing the E Dorian mode up the sixth string, then up and down the fifth string (starting on the 7th fret E). Try creating your own riffs based on this scale.

You can listen to an MP3 file of this solo on my About.com site: http://about.com/guitar/audioloudlove.

The great alto saxophonist Cannonball Adderly was a part of Miles Davis's band during a period when Davis wrote many songs based on modes. The fourth example of the site (transcribed for guitar) features Adderly playing ideas based on the G Dorian mode, over a G minor chord. Note the interesting way Adderly plays one little phrase, then jumps up to another point in the scale and plays a little phrase, and then jumps up again in the scale for the next little phrase.

This is a great one to listen to. You can listen to an MP3 file of this solo on my About.com site: http://about.com/guitar/audiomile stones.

How to Use and Practice the Dorian Mode Now that we've learned some of the performance basics of the Dorian mode, it's time to tackle a tricky subject—how to go about using it. Toward this end it's helpful to understand how the Dorian mode relates to the major scale (see **Figure 11–5** on following page).

If we were to write out the notes in these scales, here is what we'd find: The G major scale has the notes G A B C D E F♯. The A Dorian mode has the notes A B C D E F♯ G. You'll notice that both scales share exactly the same notes, which means that playing a G major scale or an A Dorian scale will result in the same sound.

Figure 11–5   G Major scale = A Dorian mode

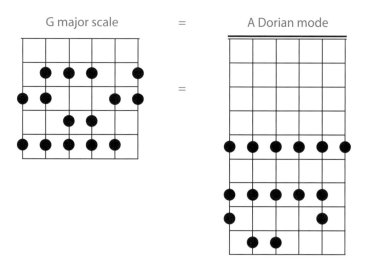

G major scale   =   A Dorian mode

To illustrate this, listen to an MP3 file of both the G major scale and the A Dorian mode being played over a G major chord on my About.com site: http://about.com/guitar/audiogmajoradorian.

Notice that both scales sound the same—the only difference being that the A Dorian scale begins and ends on the note A.

We established earlier that you can play a Dorian mode over a minor chord. Now that we know the Dorian mode is simply a major scale starting on the second note, we also know that we can use both scale patterns to give us a Dorian sound. For example, let's say we wanted to solo over an A minor chord using an A Dorian mode. Since we also know that A Dorian = G major, we know that we can use the G major scale to solo over an A minor chord. Similarly, we can use an A Dorian scale to solo over a G major chord.

The notes G and A are used just as one example. The above rules apply to all major scales—the Dorian mode starts on the second note of any major scale. So, the D Dorian mode comes from the C major scale, the G Dorian mode comes from the F major scale, etc.

In terms of how to practice the Dorian mode, it will first be necessary to completely memorize the Dorian mode pattern. Practice the mode slowly and accurately, both across the neck in the closed fingering pattern, and up a single string. Be sure to play the mode forwards and backwards in both positions.

It's important to start blurring the lines between the major scale shape and the Dorian shape on your fingerboard. Since the major scale and the Dorian mode that begins on the second degree of the major scale have all the same notes, you should try to start viewing them as one option. To start getting comfortable moving back and forth between the major scale and Dorian positions, practice the following (see **Figure 11–6**).

The idea here is, you play the ascending G major scale, then move your fretting hand up to the A Dorian position (same notes as G major), and descend in that position. You complete the scale by returning to your original position to play the final note G. After you've mastered this, you can take this concept to the next level. Try starting in the major scale position, and switching up to the Dorian

Figure 11–6   Ascending G Major, descending A Dorian pattern

position on one of the middle strings, all the while maintaining your tempo and flow. Then try something similar while descending.

You can listen to an MP3 file of this scale pattern on my About .com site: http://about.com/guitar/audiogmajortoadorian.

Once, you've got the scale under your fingers, you can start trying to improvise using the Dorian / major scale patterns. For this purpose I've provided a rhythm guitar track of an A minor vamp for you to practice along with. You can listen to an MP3 file of this A minor vamp on my About.com site: http://about.com/guitar/audio aminorvamp.

Practice playing your G major / A Dorian scale positions over the vamp. Then, try making up licks similar to the ones we studied in this chapter, by Santana and others. I recommend you spend a lot of time with this exercise, allowing your creativity to roam. Try mixing in some A minor pentatonic, A blues scale, A Dorian, and any other minor scales you know into your solos—don't feel like you have to stick with one scale throughout!

By the way, don't worry if your solos don't sound inspiring at first. Getting comfortable with a new scale takes time, and certainly won't yield wonderful results immediately. This is why we practice—so that by the time you find yourself playing it in front of others, you've got it together!

If this whole modes concept is still fuzzy to you, don't worry too much. Just practice, practice, and after that I recommend you practice some more. Chances are you'll stumble upon the logic of modes by yourself as you reflect on these exercises. Don't get frustrated if things aren't "clicking" every day—they will with time.

The Phrygian Dominant Scale

Here's a very cool sounding scale that doesn't get used a whole lot by guitarists. Not only can this scale be used for playing great solos, it also works well as the basis for guitar riffs to create whole songs around.

Before we get started working on how to play and use the Phrygian Dominant, we should make sure we understand what the scale sounds like. You can listen to an MP3 file of an A Phrygian Dominant scale on my About.com site: http://about.com/guitar/audiophrygian.

You'll note that this scale has a very Middle Eastern quality. It is a logical scale choice for rock guitarists looking to impart that flavor to their music.

Figure 11–7 shows the notes in a D Phrygian Dominant scale. The unusually large interval between the second and third notes of the scale is what gives the scale much of its characteristic sound. Note that the words "tone" and "semitone" in **Figure 11–7** are other words for whole step and half step.

Try playing this scale on one string, starting on the open fourth (D) string. Another alternative would be to start the scale on the third (G) string at the seventh fret, using the open D string as a **drone** (a note that sounds constantly) as you play both strings at once. This creates a mesmerizing effect as each note in the scale creates a different interval relative to the drone.

Your goal should be to memorize the distance between each note in the scale, so you can play it on any string, in any key.

Figure 11–7 Phrygian Dominant scale with ties and tones

D	Eb	F#	G	A	Bb	C	D
ST	T + ST	ST	T	ST	T	T	

T = tone = 2 frets   ST = semitone = 1 fret

Once you understand the concept of the Phrygian Dominant scale, try playing it with closed left hand fingering, as shown in **Figure 11–8**.

This is a tricky scale that requires a bit of finger stretching to play properly. Start with your first finger on the root of the sixth string, and play the scale slowly and evenly. Your first finger should play both the first and second notes on the fifth string (stretch your finger down one fret to play the first note on the string, then slide it back to "home" position to play the second note). The rest of the scale is fairly self explanatory, just be sure to play it accurately, forwards and backwards. The two bracketed notes on the first string indicate usable scale notes that go beyond the two-octave scale pattern. Play the notes on the last string using your first, second, and fourth fingers (that last note will require a fourth finger stretch).

Now let's take a look at how the Phrygian Dominant scale is used. **Figure 11–9** illustrates the **diatonic chords** for the D Phrygian Dominant scale. The diatonic chords of a scale are the chords that can be built using only the notes of that scale.

Playing through these chords will probably be less than inspirational for songwriting purposes, because the Phrygian Dominant scale doesn't provide a set of diatonic chords nearly as nice and tidy as the major scale. Songwriters generally have the most success, when writing songs around the Phrygian Dominant, by sticking to the root major chord, or by alternating between the root and the bII major chord (the diatonic chord built on the second note of the scale), in this case D major and E♭ major.

Experimentation is the key here. Try putting your guitar into open D tuning (DADF♯AD) and playing up the Phrygian Dominant scale on the first string, while strumming all six strings. Now, try to create a riff using the scale. Try it a few times, and you'll get the hang of it. In this situation you're using the sixth through second

Figure 11–8   Phrygian Dominant scale

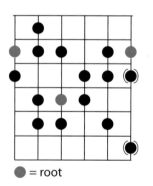

● = root

Figure 11–9   Phrygian Dominant diatonic chords

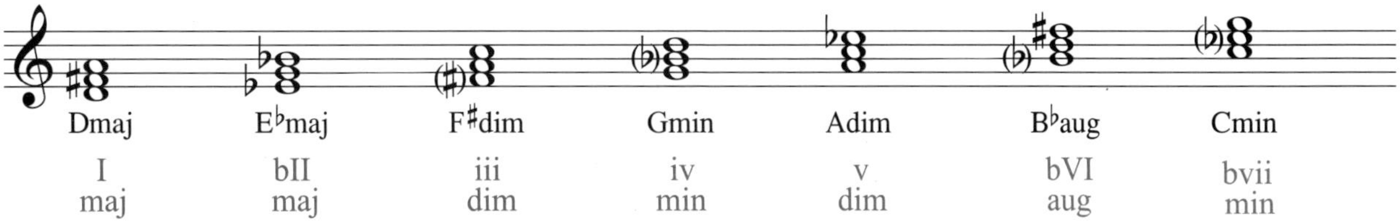

Dmaj	E♭maj	F♯dim	Gmin	Adim	B♭aug	Cmin
I	bII	iii	iv	v	bVI	bvii
maj	maj	dim	min	dim	aug	min

strings as drone strings to accompany your improvisation on the first string. This is big fun!

When used for soloing purposes (in a pop / rock context), the Phrygian Dominant scale also usually works best in situations where a chord progression lingers, or vamps, on a single major chord for relatively long period of time. It is a very distinct and strong sounding scale, so it has the potential to sound very out of place against many other chord progressions.

In a jazz context, this scale gets used in a much different situation; generally on a V7 chord (a dominant seventh chord built on the fifth note of the scale of the key you're playing in), to create an altered dominant sound. For example, on the progression G7 to C major 7, the G Phrygian Dominant scale would be played on the G7 chord, to create a G7♭9 sound, which resolves nicely to the C major 7. The Phrygian Dominant scale is also used on V7 chords in minor keys (G7 to C minor).

Keep practicing, experimenting and jamming with the Phrygian Dominant scale—it will eventually yield some very interesting and exciting additions to your soloing repertoire.

Canadian band The Tea Party was one group that used the Phrygian Dominant scale extensively in the creation of their "Moroccan Roll," a blend of progressive rock and Middle Eastern influences and instrumentation. Check out their popular album Transmission (Atlantic 1997) on the Tower Records website, where you can listen to short samples of every track. The first track, "Temptation," is a great example of what happens when rock dynamics and Middle Eastern scales meet. Just go to www.towerrecords.com/product. aspx?pfid=1204945&title=Transmission+*&artist=The+Tea+Party.

Strumming Pattern with Bass Line

In Chapter 10 we started learning how to incorporate bass notes into our strumming patterns. Now, we'll explore that concept further by trying to incorporate a whole **bass line** into our strumming patterns (see **Figure 11–10**).

This one will be tricky at first, but as your picking accuracy increases, it'll sound better and better. In your fretting hand, hold down a G major chord, with your second finger on the sixth string, first finger on the fifth string, and third finger on the first string. Now, strike the sixth string with your pick, and follow that by down-and-up strums on the bottom four strings of the chord. Follow the tablature in **Figure 11–10** to complete the rest of the pattern.

When you've finished playing the pattern once, keep looping it multiple times. Be sure to keep your picking motion constant, whether you're playing a single note or strumming a chord. If you're too deliberate while playing the single notes, it will break up the flow of your strum, and the resulting pattern will sound choppy.

Figure 11–10   G major strum

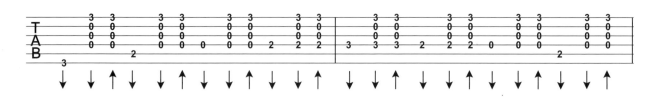

You can hear this strumming pattern in G major, first slowly and then more **uptempo**, on my About.com site: http://about.com/guitar/audiostrumgmajor.

The next strum is somewhat tricky but should really help you work on your picking accuracy. You'll note that this strum also incorporates a hammer-on in the fretting hand (see **Figure 11–11**).

Begin by holding down a D major chord in your fretting hand. Play the fourth string with a downstroke, and follow that by strumming the remaining three notes in the chord with a down-up strum. Now play the open fifth string, followed again by a down-up strum of the remaining three notes. Play the open fourth string again, followed by a down-up strum. Now take your first finger off the third string, play it open, and then hammer your first finger back onto the second fret. Finish with another down-up strum, and you've completed the pattern. Try it until you get the hang of it, and then loop the pattern. It will seem much less complex in no time.

You can hear this strumming pattern in D major, first slowly and then more uptempo, on my About.com site: http://about.com/guitar/audiostrumdmajor.

Here are some things to remember:

- It is extremely important, when playing the patterns explained in this chapter, to keep your strumming motion constant, whether you're playing the single notes or the full chords.

Figure 11–11   D major strum

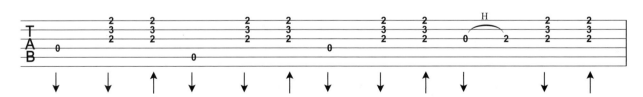

- You might find that at first you accidentally play several strings when trying to strum one string. Don't get upset—just try to remedy the problem.
- When hammering-on, make sure that both the initial and the hammered-on notes ring clearly.
- These new strums are rather complex, but don't sweat it! You'll get the hang of it quickly!

Introduction to Sus4 Chords

Now let's look at a new type of chord—the sus4 (short for "suspended fourth") chord.

Sus4 chords (pronounced "suss four") have a different construction than the other chords we've studied. Instead of being built with the first, third, and fifth notes of the scale, they're built with the first, fourth, and fifth.

Sus4 chords are often (but not always) used in combination with a major or minor chord of the same letter name. For example, it's common to see the chord progression D major–Dsus4–D major. Or you might see something like this: Asus4–A minor. As you learn these chords, try playing them and then following each with a major or minor chord of the same letter name.

This Asus4 chord (see **Figure 11–12**) is one that you can fret in several ways, depending on which other chords you're playing. You can fret the fourth, third, and second strings with your second, third, and fourth fingers, which makes it easy to change to an open A minor chord. Or you can fret the chord with a first-finger barre across the fourth and third string and use your second finger to fret the second string, making it easy to switch to an A major chord. Or you can fret those strings with your first, second, and third fingers, making it easy to change to a D major chord. Note that **Figure 11–12** tells you not to play the sixth string. When you practice, change among all three of these fingerings of the Asus4 chord—it's an interesting study of how you can use different finger combinations to play the exact same chord.

Try these changes:

- A major to Asus4 to A major
- D major to Asus4 to D major
- A minor to Asus4 to A minor

As you can see from the Xs over the sixth and first strings in **Figure 11–13**, this Csus4 chord presents a picking challenge. You have to be careful not to strum the sixth or first strings when playing this chord, which will take some practice. (One alternative is to reach in and pluck the four middle strings all at one time with your thumb and first three fingers.) Use your third finger to play the note on the fifth string, your fourth finger to play the note on the fourth string, and your first finger to play the note on the second string.

Try these changes:

- C major to Csus4 to C major
- D minor to Csus4 to C major

This Dsus4 chord is a common chord. If going from Dsus4 to D major, use your first finger on the third string, your third finger on the second string, and your fourth finger on the first string. If going from Dsus4 to D minor, try your second finger on the third string, your third finger on the second string, and your fourth finger on the first string (see **Figure 11–14** on following page).

Try these changes:

- Dsus4 to D minor
- D major to Dsus4 to D major
- D major to D minor to Dsus4

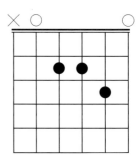

Figure 11–12   Asus4 chord

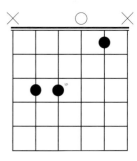

Figure 11–13   Csus4 chord

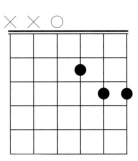

Figure 11–14   Dsus4 chord

Figure 11–15   Esus4 chord

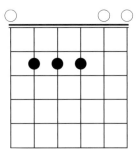

Figure 11–16   Fsus4 chord

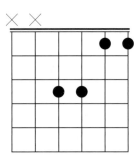

Try playing this Esus4 chord with your second finger on the fifth string, your third finger on the fourth string, and your fourth finger on the third string. You could also try first finger on fifth string, second finger on fourth, and third finger on third, in the shape of an A major chord (see **Figure 11–15**).

Try these changes:

- Esus4 to E major
- E minor to Esus4 to E minor
- A major to Esus4 to A major

Play this Fsus4 chord by placing your third finger on the fourth string, your fourth finger on the third string, and your first finger on the remaining two strings. The diagram has Xs over the sixth and fifth strings, so be careful to only play the bottom four strings (see **Figure 11–16**).

Try these changes:

- F major to Fsus4 to F major
- C major to Fsus4 to F major

Pay attention to the X over the fifth string on this Gsus4 chord—that string should not be played. Use your third finger (which is playing the note on the sixth string) to lightly touch the fifth string so it doesn't ring. Your first finger should play the note on the second string, while your fourth finger plays the note on the first string (see **Figure 11–17**).

Try these changes:

- Gsus4 to G major
- A minor to Gsus4 to G major
- Gsus4 to G major to Csus4 to C major

Like all barre chords, we can learn one chord shape and move it around to create many more sus4 chords. **Figure 11–18** illustrates the basic shape of the sus4 chord with the root on the sixth string. When playing the chord, be aware that the notes on the second and first strings are optional, and don't need to be played. You can try playing this chord shape by barring with your first finger, then playing the note on the fifth string with your second finger, the fourth string with the third finger, and the third string with the fourth finger. Alternately, you could try playing the sixth string with your first finger, barring the fifth, fourth, and third strings with your third finger, and avoid playing the second and first strings.

Try these changes:

- Bsus4 to B major
- F♯sus4 to F♯ minor
- Dsus4 to D major to Gsus4 to G major

Figure 11–19 illustrates the basic shape of the sus4 chord with the root on the fifth string. When playing this voicing, be aware that the note on the first string is optional, and is often left off. You can finger this chord shape by putting your first finger on the fifth string (and optionally the first string as well), your second finger on the fourth string, your third finger on the third string, and your fourth finger on the second string. Alternately, you could try playing the fifth string with your first finger, barring the fourth and third strings with your third finger, and playing the second string with your fourth finger.

Try these changes:

- Esus4 to E major
- C♯sus4 to C♯ minor
- Gsus4 to G major to Fsus4 to F major

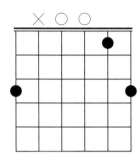

Figure 11–17   Gsus4 chord

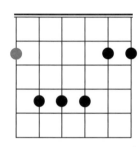

Figure 11–18   6th string sus4 barre chord

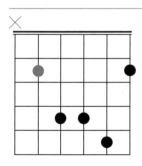

Figure 11–19   5th string sus4 barre chord

Here are some things you should know:

- Sus4 chords are also commonly referred to simply as "sus" or "suspended" chords.
- Sus4 chords tend to feel "unresolved" if left hanging, so you probably wouldn't want to end a song on a sus4 chord.
- Many guitarists insert sus4 chords into music with simple major and minor chords, to spice up a guitar part.

Songs You Can Play Now

These songs incorporate the techniques that we studied in this chapter.

○ "The Needle and the Damage Done," *Neil Young*
www.chordie.com/chord.pere?url=http://getsome.org/guitar/olga/chordpro/y/Neil.Young/TheNeedleAndTheDamageDone.chopro

○ "Happy Xmas (War Is Over)," *John Lennon*
www.chordie.com/chord.pere/www.ultimate-guitar.com/print.php?what=tab&id=273066

○ "You've Got to Hide Your Love Away," *the Beatles*
www.chordie.com/chord.pere/www.ultimate-guitar.com/print.php?what=tab&id=60715

○ "The Man Who Sold the World," *David Bowie / Nirvana*
www.chordie.com/chord.pere/www.ultimate-guitar.com/print.php?what=tab&id=155727

When you practice, take the time to go back over the previous chapters. We have covered a vast amount of material, so it's highly doubtful that you will remember how to play everything you've

▶▶▶
"The Needle and the Damage Done" uses the strumming pattern with bass line concept. "Happy Xmas (War Is Over)" and "You've Got to Hide Your Love Away" have sus4 chords in their progressions. Note that "Happy Christmas (War Is Over)" and "You've Got to Hide Your Love Away" are waltzes (counted 1-2-3, 1-2-3) so use this strumming pattern: down, down-up, down-up.

learned without some review. After you've done that, focus on these points:

1. Make sure your guitar is in tune.
2. Download one of the software versions of a metronome, either KeepTime or Drone, and use it to practice with. Here are the links:

   www.audioplayer.com/smm/programs/KeepTime/download.shtml

   www.audioplayer.com/smm/programs/Drone/download.shtml

3. Practice the major scale, using the metronome to keep time (pick a tempo you're comfortable with).
4. Review barre chords we've covered. Also, go over your new sus4 chords. Pay attention to how similar sus4 chords are to major chords with the same letter name.
5. Practice the new advanced strumming patterns. They'll take some work, but you're going to want to incorporate these concepts into your strumming, so it's worth your time.
6. Try some string bends, slides, hammer-ons, and pull-offs whenever you play guitar. Try playing your scales with these techniques.
7. Keep practicing the fingerpicking patterns from Chapters 9 and 10, and the songs from those lessons that use them.
8. Try to play all of the songs listed in this chapter, and also keep playing those from previous lessons.

If you're feeling confident with everything you've learned so far, try to find a few songs you're interested in, and learn them on your own. You can use the easy song tabs archive, the greatest albums tab and lyrics archive, or the guitar tab area of my About.com site to hunt down the music that you'd enjoy learning the most. You'll find the links in the next section. Try memorizing some of these songs, rather than always looking at the music to play them.

Get Linked

You can find information about subjects above and beyond what we've discussed in these chapters on my **About.com** *site. Check out this interesting link.*

GREATEST ALBUMS
ARCHIVE

Greatest album tab and lyrics archive

http://about.com/guitar/greatestalbums

Chapter 12

Palm Muting and Chord Inversions

Introduction to Palm Muting

Palm muting is a guitar technique that's executed by the picking hand. The base of the palm is used to muffle the strings slightly while you pluck the strings with the pick. It's a technique that's used very effectively on electric guitar, and it also serves a useful role when you're playing acoustic guitar.

You can hear an excerpt from Weezer's "Hash Pipe" that demonstrates the sound of palm muting on my About.com site: http://about.com/guitar/audiopalmmuting. If you're near your computer, check out the clip now.

Can you hear how the guitar sounds slightly "subdued" at the beginning? That's the result of palm muting. If you listen carefully, you'll note that near the end of the clip, the band stops palm muting the guitar, and the music gets louder, with a more unrestrained feeling. This is one common use for palm muting—if part of the song is played with palm-muted guitar, the part that's not muted seems louder and more aggressive than it otherwise would have. Note that palm muting is used in many styles of music, so even if the Weezer clip didn't appeal to you, the technique is still worth learning.

The concept is to slightly mute the notes you are hitting with the pick, yet not mute them so much that the notes can't be heard. Do this by resting the heel of your picking hand lightly on the strings, close to the bridge of the guitar. With your fretting hand, position your fingers to play an A power chord with the root on the sixth string. Now, with the heel of your hand still touching all relevant strings (make sure it's covering the sixth, fifth, and fourth strings—the ones we're going to play), use your pick to play the chord. In a perfect world, you'd hear all the notes in the chord, though they'd be slightly muffled. Chances are, though, the first time you try it, it won't sound wonderful.

Getting a proper feel for how much pressure to apply with the heel of your picking hand is the key to this technique. If you apply too much pressure, the notes won't ring at all. Apply uneven pressure, and some notes will sound muted, while others will ring out too much. To find the sweet spot, start by moving the heel of your palm behind the bridge so the strings aren't muted at all. Then, while strumming an even rhythm, slowly move the heel of your hand forward over the bridge until the sound of the strings becomes constrained and rubbery while their notes are still present. If the strings sound flat and it's hard to distinguish their notes, you've moved too far forward. Try this a couple of times and you'll find the spot that sounds good. Concentrate on getting a very even, controlled sound whenever you attempt palm muting.

For further illustration of how palm muting is supposed to sound, you can listen to a clip of an A5 chord (A power chord) being played first with palm muting, then without, on my About. com site: http://about.com/guitar/audioa5chord.

Things to remember:

- Let the flesh on the heel of your palm do all the work. Experiment with your hand position until it feels comfortable on the strings. This is a technique that is easy once you get it, but can be frustrating to learn.
- Practice this technique a lot. Palm muting is used all the time in many styles of music.
- Concentrate on palm muting when playing power chords. This is where the technique is used almost constantly by many guitarists.
- Listen for palm muting in your favorite music. Once you learn to recognize it, you'll start to realize how often this technique is used.
- Make sure your muting hand isn't too far up the guitar (toward the headstock). The farther up the guitar your hand is, the easier it will be to accidentally mute the strings completely.

Introduction to Major Chord Inversions

At this point, you've learned to play an A major chord three ways—the open A major chord, and the two barre chord shapes (one with its root on the sixth string, and one with its root on the fifth string). If you remember all three shapes, that's terrific! But I've got news for you—there are many more ways to play an A major, or any other major chord.

A major chord is made up of three notes only: the root, the major third, and the fifth. If any other notes are added, the name of the chord changes to something else (such as a major 7 chord, or a major 6 chord). Even though we strum more than three notes in all of our major chords, if you check each of the notes you'll find that there are only three different notes being played, and that the other strings are simply repeated notes in different octaves.

The major chords we will explore in this chapter leave out any such repeated notes, so only three strings are played in each chord. First we'll look at major chords grouped on the sixth, fifth, and fourth strings.

Figure 12–1   6-5-4 string major chord inversions

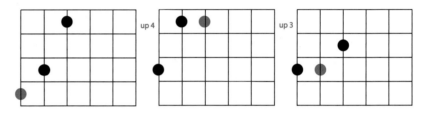

These three chord shapes are all different inversions of the exact same chord, meaning that while they contain the same notes, the notes occur in a different order. These inversions are also called different "voicings" of the chord. In each diagram in **Figure 12–1**, the root of the chord is indicated in red.

The first step in playing these three chord shapes will be to find the root note of the major chord you want to play on the sixth string. For this exercise we'll play A major chords, so the root will be on the fifth fret. Play the first chord voicing shown in **Figure 12–1** using your fourth finger on the sixth string, third finger on the fifth string, and first finger on the fourth string. This is referred to as a **root position** major chord because the root note is the lowest note sounding in the chord.

To play the second chord illustrated in **Figure 12–1**, count up four frets from the root of the first chord. This fret (the ninth) will be the starting note of the chord shape. Use your third finger to play the note on the sixth string and your first finger to barre the fifth and fourth strings. This type of chord is referred to as a **first** inversion major chord, because the root note has been taken from the bottom and moved to the top. Try moving back and forth between the root position and first inversion chord. Eventually you'll get a feel for the distance between the two chords and will be able to move from voicing to voicing without counting frets.

To play the last chord voicing illustrated in **Figure 12–1**, count up three frets on the sixth string from the last chord you played, and start the new voicing on that fret (the twelfth). Use your third finger on the sixth string, second finger on the fifth string, and first finger on the fourth string. This type of chord is referred to as a **second inversion** major chord, because the third has been taken from the bottom and moved to the top.

If you would like to bring these voicings full circle, you can count up five more frets on the sixth string, and play the root position chord again starting on the seventeenth fret.

Once you've memorized these chord shapes, try moving back and forth between all three chord voicings for the A major chord, or whatever chord you've chosen to practice on any given day.

Now we'll look at major chords grouped on the fifth, fourth, and third strings.

Figure 12–2   5-4-3 string major chord inversions

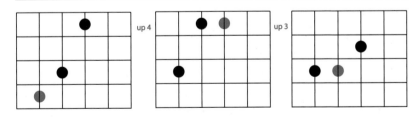

If you look at the diagrams in **Figure 12–2**, you'll see that they're exactly the same shapes as the chords in **Figure 12–1**, which were

How can I learn all these chord inversions?

▶ Trying to learn and use these new chord shapes is a daunting task at first. The thought of picking up a guitar and playing a first inversion A major chord—which doesn't even have the root on the bottom—seems impossible. The key to using chord inversions properly is to know which string the root is on in each voicing you play. When you combine this with your knowledge of the names of the notes on the sixth and fifth strings, you'll be able to form these chord shapes around any root you want.

formed on the sixth, fifth, and fourth strings. That means if you apply the rules discussed in the previous section to the chord shapes in **Figure 12–2**, you'll have three more ways to play a major chord.

Once you're comfortable with the chords on string groups 6-5-4 and 5-4-3, try substituting those shapes to play the major chords in progressions you're playing. Since all of the major chord voicings you just learned have the same notes as "normal" major chords, you could theoretically insert any of them at any time you were required to play a major chord.

This is where personal preference becomes your guide. Some guitarists will elect to use these shapes all the time, while others will use them more sparingly.

As you become more familiar with these chord voicings, you'll figure out how and when to use them. If you're the only guitarist accompanying a group of people singing, you wouldn't want to choose the A major chord shape on the sixteenth fret of the fifth string, amidst a bunch of other "normal" open chords. In that situation, you'd want the full sound of open chords. But if you were the second guitar in that same situation, your role would be different. In that situation you could let the other guitarist play the open chords, and you could use some of these new inversions. They would add a nice, fuller sound to the music.

Whenever you're playing, you'll need to let the musical situation dictate whether or not to use these major chord inversions.

More Major Chord Inversions

Now we'll learn the major chord inversions for the last two string groups, 4-3-2 and 3-2-1.

The concept of playing the major chord inversions on the 4-3-2 string group is exactly the same as it was for the previous groups.

To play the root position chord, find the root note of the major chord you want to play on the fourth string of the guitar. If you're not yet familiar with the names of the notes on the fourth string, here's a tip: Find the root on the sixth string—the same note is two frets higher on the fourth string. Now play the first chord in **Figure 12–3**, fingered as follows: third finger on the fourth string, second finger on the third string, and first finger on the second string.

To play the first inversion major chord on this string group, you'll either need to locate the chord root on the second string and form the chord around that, or count up four frets on the fourth string to the next voicing. The fingering is close to the root position chord—just switch your middle finger to the second string, and your index finger to the third string.

To play the second inversion of the major chord, you'll need to find the chord root on the third string, or count up three frets on the fourth string from the first inversion chord shape. If you're not yet familiar with the names of the notes on the third string, find the root on the fifth string—the same note is two frets higher on the third string. This last voicing can be played any number of ways: with the first, second, and third fingers, with the second, third, and fourth fingers, or just by barring all three notes with the first finger.

Figure 12–3   4-3-2 string group major chords

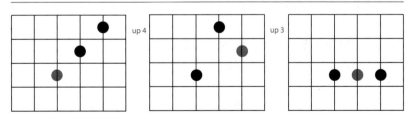

Let's play the voicings of an A major chord on the 4-3-2 string group as an exercise. The root position chord starts on the seventh fret of the fourth string. The first inversion chord starts on the eleventh fret of the fourth string. Finally, the second inversion chord starts on the fourteenth fret of the fourth string—or it can be played down the octave at the second fret, in the open position.

Now let's look at the last string group.

To play the root position chord on the 3-2-1 string group, find the root of the chord you'd like to play on the third string. If you're not yet familiar with the names of the notes on the third string, find the root on the fifth string—the same note is two frets higher on the third string. Now play the root position chord with your third finger on the third string, fourth finger on the second string, and first finger on the first string.

To play the first inversion major chord in **Figure 12–4**, either locate the chord root on the first string and form the chord around that, or count up four frets on the third string to the next voicing. Play the first inversion chord with your second finger on the third string, and with your first finger barring the second and first strings.

Figure 12–4   3-2-1 string group major chords

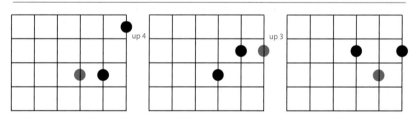

The second inversion major chord in **Figure 12–4** can be played either by finding the chord root on the second string, or by counting up three frets on the third string from the previous chord shape. Play this voicing using your first finger on the third string, your third finger on the second string, and your second finger on the first string.

Let's play the voicings of a D major chord on the 3-2-1 string group as an exercise. The root position chord starts on the seventh fret of the third string. The first inversion chord starts on the eleventh fret of the third string. Finally, the second inversion chord starts on the fourteenth fret of the third string—or it can be played down the octave at the second fret, in the open position.

Things to try:

- Start by playing just the root position chord on both of the string groups we studied (4-3-2 strings and 3-2-1 strings).
- Play the root position, first inversion, and second inversion chords on both of the string groups.
- Play the root position voicing of a G major chord, then the root position voicing of a D major chord on the 4-3-2 string group. Repeat on the 3-2-1 group.
- Play the root position voicing of a C major chord on the 4-3-2 string group, then move directly to the closest voicing on the same string group of an F major chord, whether it's root position, first inversion, or second inversion. Repeat this on the 3-2-1 string group.

Advanced String Bending

In Chapter 10 we got into the basics of string bending, learning to do half-step and whole-step versions of the bend and release. Now we'll add a couple of other vital bending techniques.

Figure 12–5 shows three variations of a very simple guitar riff used often by legendary blues guitarist B.B. King. We'll use this phrase to illustrate the various types of bending.

The first bending technique in **Figure 12–5**, the **bend and release**, is the one you learned in Chapter 10. Bend the note up a whole step and bring it back to its original pitch. Then play the second note of the riff on the eighth fret.

The second technique in **Figure 12–5** is generally just referred to as a **string bend**. This time, instead of bending the pitch and then audibly bringing it back to its original pitch, we mute the string while it is still bent, so you don't hear the string returning to its original pitch. You accomplish this by hitting the string with a downstroke, bending the note up a whole step and then, at the top of the bend, touching the still-bent string with your pick or finger to cause it to stop ringing. As soon as it does, you release the bent string back to its original position and play the second note of the riff.

The third technique on the tab in **Figure 12–5** is called a **pre-bend**. The pre-bend differs in that you bend the string before you play it. Bend the tenth fret of the second string up a whole step, and then hit the string with your pick. As the note sounds, release the bend so the pitch audibly returns to normal, and play the second note.

Figure 12–5   Types of bends

The **ABOUT.com** *Guide to* **Acoustic Guitar**

The pre-bend can be a little tricky because you have to estimate how far to bend the note without being able to hear it. Practice bending the note up a whole step while plucking the note to get used to the correct tension of the bend, and then start bending up the string silently and plucking the note at the top of the bend. You'll get it quickly.

You can listen to an MP3 file of each of these three string bends on my About.com site: http://about.com/guitar/audiostringbends.

Songs You Can Play Now

We learned quite a bit about specific guitar techniques this chapter. Let's try to put some of these principles into practice, while still having some fun!

- ○ "Hash Pipe," *Weezer*
  www.geocities.com/etheltheaardvark/weezerhashpipe.txt

- ○ "Better Be Home Soon," *Crowded House*
  www.etext.org/lists/house/ct/better-be-home-soon-CT.html

- ○ "Desperado," *the Eagles*
  www.geocities.com/etheltheaardvark/desperado.txt

- ○ "Stairway to Heaven," *guitar solo by Jimmy Page / Led Zeppelin*
  www.olga.net/archive/main/l/led_zeppelin/stairway_solo.
  tab?printer=0

You know the basic practice drill by now. We have covered a vast amount of material, so I hope you're increasing your daily practice time accordingly. At this point an hour a day would be appropriate, and it should go by pretty quickly with all the exercises you have to fill it.

◀◀◀
"Hash Pipe," as you'll recall, uses a lot of palm muting as well as power chords, also known as fifth chords. "Better Be Home Soon" includes some seven chords and one slash chord, and "Desperado" uses a bunch of seven chords.

Here's how to get started:

1. Make sure your guitar is in tune.
2. Download one of the software versions of a metronome, and use it to practice with. Here are the links:

   www.audioplayer.com/smm/programs/KeepTime/down load.shtml

   www.audioplayer.com/smm/programs/Drone/down load.shtml

3. Practice scales you've learned, using the metronome to keep time. Try palm muting the scale. Try sliding from note to note. Try hammering on as you ascend the scale, and pulling off as you descend.
4. Do some string bending. Do this often, because you won't get better at it until you build up some finger strength. Even if you hate doing it, try doing it for one or two minutes every time you play the guitar. You'll be happy you did.
5. Keep practicing the fingerpicking patterns from Chapters 9 and 10.
6. Try to play all of the songs listed in this chapter, and keep playing those from previous lessons.
7. Practice this chapter's major chord inversions using the special section that follows. We're going to keep studying these in detail, so it's important to get the basics together.

Let's focus on this special practice section on chord inversions, which is designed to help you learn these new chords quickly.

Exercise 1

Randomly choose a major chord to work with. You might choose A major or C major to try these little games:

1. Start by playing only the root position chord on both of the string groups we studied (6-5-4 strings and 5-4-3 strings).
2. Next, play root position, first inversion, and second inversion chords on both of the string groups.
3. If space allows, try playing the chords **down the neck** starting with the root position. For example, play A major on the 5-4-3 string grouping, with the root position at twelfth fret; then second inversion on seventh fret; and finally, first inversion on the fourth fret.
4. Next, try picturing the root position chord shape on each string group, without playing it. Then, play each first inversion shape.
5. Picture the root position and first inversion chord shapes on each string group, without playing them. Then play each second inversion shape.
6. Play the first inversion major chord shapes on both string groups, without playing the root position chord.
7. Repeat Step 6 with second inversion chords.

Exercise 2

Choose two major chords. It may be easier to begin with if the chords are in the same key. Use one of the following pairs of chords: C major and F major; D major and A major; G major and C major; B♭ major and F major; E major and A major; or G major and D major. Now try these little two-chord games:

1. Play the root position voicing of the first chord, and then the root position voicing of the second chord. Repeat on the second string group.

2. Play the root position voicing of the first chord, and then the root position, first inversion, and second inversion voicings for the second chord. Repeat on the second string group. While you are playing the voicings for the second chord, remember where you played the root position voicing for the first chord.

3. Play the root position voicing for the first chord, then move directly to the closest voicing on the same string group for the second chord, whether it is root position, first inversion, or second inversion. Repeat on each string group.

4. Play the first inversion voicing for the first chord, and then move directly to the closest voicing on the same string group for the second chord, whether it is root position, first inversion, or second inversion. Repeat on each string group.

5. Repeat Step 4 above for the second inversion voicing of the first chord on each string group.

6. Play the lowest voicing available on a string group for the first voicing (whether that is the root position, first inversion, or second inversion). Move up the neck to the closest available inversion for the second chord. Move up the neck again to the next available inversion of the first chord. Repeat this process all the way up the neck, on each string group.

These chord inversion games will teach your fingers to move from voicing to voicing quickly and fluidly. If you practice these games (or any others you care to invent yourself), playing these chord changes will become so natural and so much second-nature that you'll barely have to think about them.

Get Linked

*You can find information about subjects above and beyond what we've had time to discuss in these chapters on my **About.com** site. Because we looked at palm muting in this chapter I thought you'd be interested in exploring a form of music that uses this technique extensively— funk music. Funk also requires a lot of muting or string deadening in the fretting hand to create its rhythmic staccato guitar parts. Check out this interesting link.*

FUNK MUSIC PRIMER

Four-part lesson on playing funk music on guitar

http://about.com/guitar/funklesson

Chapter 13

Seventh Chords and Advanced Strumming

Introduction to Seventh Barre Chords

The major and minor barre chords with roots on the sixth and fifth strings that you've learned will take you a long way—you can play thousands of songs using only these chord shapes, as you've probably guessed by the broad range of songs listed at the end of each chapter. However, there are many more types of chords available to us that will add rich color to the sound of our progressions.

This is another situation where you'll need to know the names of notes on sixth and fifth strings. If you aren't completely familiar with them, set aside a few minutes of your practice time every day for studying and memorizing them. It shouldn't take you long to learn them by heart.

Let's look now at three types of seventh barre chords, beginning with the **major seventh chord**. Let's start by using the note C as an example. Its major seventh chord is written as Cmaj7, or C major 7, or sometimes CM7. The chord is built out of the root, third, fifth, and seventh notes of the scale. To the unfamiliar ear, the major seventh chord might sound a little unusual. Used in the proper context, however, it's a colorful and commonly used chord.

The chord shape with the root on the sixth string is not actually a barre chord, although it is usually labeled as such. Play it with your first finger on the sixth string, third finger on the fourth string, fourth finger on the third string, and second finger on the second string. Note the Xs above the fifth and first strings in **Figure 13–1** —be careful not to let those strings ring. One tip is to try letting your first finger lightly touch the fifth string so it doesn't ring.

Figure 13–1 Major seventh chords

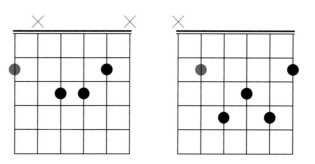

Playing the chord shape with the root on the fifth string involves barring strings five through one with your first finger. Your third finger goes on the fourth string, second finger on the third string, and fourth finger on the second string. Be sure to avoid playing the sixth string, as the X above it in **Figure 13–1** indicates.

Next we'll look at **dominant seventh chords**. Although technically referred to as a "dominant seventh chord," this type of chord is often just referred to as a "seventh chord." Using the note A as an example, this chord is written as Adom7, or A7. The difference between the dominant seventh and the major seventh chords is that the dominant seventh chord has a flatted seventh note. This chord is extremely common in all types of music.

To play the sixth-string shape, barre all six strings with your first finger. Your third finger plays the note on the fifth string, while your second finger plays the note on the third string. Check to make sure that the note on the fourth string is sounding—this is the toughest note to get to ring clearly.

Play the fifth-string shape by barring strings five through one with your first finger. Your third finger goes on the fourth string, while your fourth finger plays the note on the second string. Be careful not to play the sixth string, as the X above it in **Figure 13–2** indicates.

Figure 13–2   Dominant seventh chords

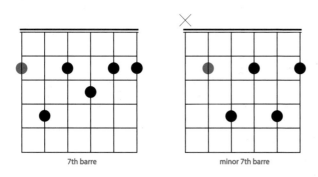

7th barre   minor 7th barre

Finally, we'll check out **minor seventh chords**. Using the note Bb as an example, this chord might be written as Bbmin7, or Bbm7, or sometimes Bb-7. It's built out of the root, flatted third, fifth, and flatted seventh notes of the scale (see **Figure 13–3**).

To play the sixth-string shape, barre all six strings with your first finger. Your third finger plays the note on the fifth string. Check to make sure that all strings are ringing clearly.

Play the fifth-string shape by barring strings five through one with your first finger. Your third finger goes on the fourth string, while your second finger plays note on the second string. Be careful not to play the sixth string, as the X above it in **Figure 13-3** indicates.

Figure 13-3   Minor seventh chords

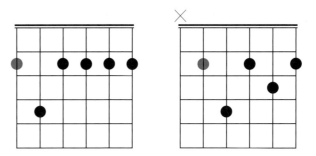

Things to try:

- Learn all six of these chords well. Remember the shape, the type, and which string the root is on.
- Call out a random chord (say Gmin7). Now, see how quickly you can play it with the root on the sixth and fifth strings.
- When you're playing songs, try moving from one chord to the closest voicing of the next chord. For example, when playing Gmaj7 to Cmaj7, don't slide from the third fret up to the eighth fret—look for a closer option. In this case it's moving from the Gmaj7 with root on sixth, played on the third fret, to Cmaj7 with root on fifth—also on the third fret.

Introduction to Minor Chord Inversions

In Chapter 12, when we studied major chord inversions, we learned twelve ways (three on each of the four string groups) to play a major chord on the fingerboard. This same concept can be applied to minor chords.

Learning these new voicings will allow you to begin "**voice leading**" (the process of each note of a chord moving smoothly and minimally to the next chord). Once you've begun to learn the sound of voice leading, you'll find it starting to creep into your guitar solos too.

These minor chord inversions are also useful in improvising. Many guitarists (Carlos Santana and David Gilmour come to mind) often use arpeggios in their solos. Arpeggios are simply the notes in a chord played one at a time instead of all together. For example, over an A minor chord, Carlos Santana might play an arpeggio using any of the twelve A minor chord shapes we are about to learn.

Figure 13–4   6-5-4 string group minor chord inversions

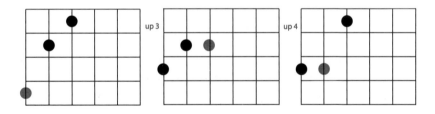

Find the root note of the minor chord you want to play on the sixth string. Then, play the first chord voicing in **Figure 13–4**, planting your fourth finger on the 6th string, second finger on the 5th string, and first finger on the 4th string. This is referred to as a root position minor chord, because the root note is the lowest note sounding in the chord.

To play the first inversion minor chord, find the root note on the fourth string, and form the chord shape around that. (Alternately, try counting up three frets from the note you played on the 6th string. This will be the starting note for the next chord shape.) Play the note on the 6th string with your second finger, and use the index finger to barre the 5th and 4th strings. Try moving back and forth between the root position and first inversion chord. Eventually, you will get a feel for how far the distance between the two are, and will be able to move from voicing to voicing without counting frets.

To play the second inversion minor chord voicing in **Figure 13–4**, you again have two options. You can find the root note on the 5th string, and form the chord around that note. Or, you can count up four frets on the 6th string from the last chord you played, and start the voicing on that fret. Play this inversion with your third finger on 6th string, fourth finger on 5th string and first finger on 4th string. If you would like to bring these voicings full-circle, count up five frets on the sixth string, and play the root position chord again.

Once you've memorized these chord shapes, try moving back and forth between all three chord voicings for the minor chord you've chosen. They should all sound similar—all three chord shapes above contain the exact same three notes. In each voicing, the three notes are simply arranged in a different order.

As an example, to play an A minor chord using the above 6-5-4 string group voicings, the root position chord starts on the 5th fret of the 6th string. The first inversion chord starts on the 8th fret of the 6th string, and the second inversion chord starts on the 12th fret of the 6th string.

As was the case when you learned major chord voicings, you'll notice that these minor chords are exactly the same shapes as those formed on the 6th, 5th, and 4th strings (see **Figure 13–5**).

So if you follow the above rules for these chord shapes you'll have learned three more ways to play a minor chord.

Figure 13–5   5-4-3 string group minor chord inversions

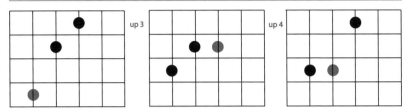

Once you're comfortable with the above chords on string groups 6-5-4 and 5-4-3, try using these same shapes to play different minor chords (like F, B♭, E, etc.)

As an example, to play an A minor chord using the above 5-4-3 string group voicings, the root position chord starts on the 12th fret of the 5th string. The first inversion chord starts on the 3rd fret of the 5th string (or the 15th fret). And the second inversion chord starts on the 7th fret of the 5th string (or the 19th fret).

More Minor Chord Inversions

Now let's look at the minor chord inversions for the last two string groups, beginning with the 4-3-2 string group (see **Figure 13–6**).

Figure 13–6   4-3-2 string group minor chord inversions

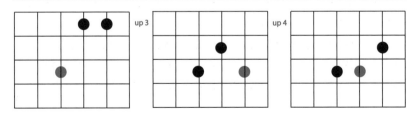

ASK YOUR GUIDE

How can I get better at making such quick chord changes?

▸ Start by using some of your most familiar open position chords—G major, E minor, C major, and D major. Count 1-2-3-4, and play one downstroke on each beat. Then switch between these four chords in order so you're playing one chord on each downstroke. Start slowly and, when you can play each chord cleanly, speed up the rhythm. This will get your fingers used to moving from one chord shape to another in one swift motion.

The concept of playing this group of chords is exactly the same as it was for the previous groups. To play the root position chord, find the root note of the minor chord on the 4th string of the guitar. If you're having trouble finding the note on the 4th string, remember our tip: Find the root on the 6th string, then count over two strings, and up two frets to find the same note one octave higher. Now play the first chord above, fingered as follows: third finger on the 4th string, and first finger barring the 3rd and 2nd strings.

To play the first inversion minor chord on this string group, you'll either need to locate the chord root on the 2nd string and form the chord around that, or count up three frets on the 4th string to the next voicing. Finger this chord as follows: second finger on the 4th string, first finger on the 3rd string, and third finger on the 2nd string.

To play the second inversion minor chord, either try to find the chord root on the 3rd string, or count up four frets on the 4th string from the previous chord shape. If you're not familiar with the notes on the 3rd string yet, find the root on the 5th string and then count over two strings, and up two frets to find the same note one octave up. This voicing can be played several ways, the most popular of which is: second finger on the 4th string, third finger on the 3rd string and first finger on the 2nd string.

As an example, to play an A minor chord using the above 4-3-2 string group voicings, the root position chord starts on the 7th fret of the 4th string. The first inversion chord starts on the 10th fret of the 4th string. And the second inversion chord starts on the 14th fret of the 4th string (or it could be played down the octave at the 2nd fret.)

Let's move on to the final string group (see **Figure 13–7**). Start by finding the root of the chord you want to play on the 3rd string (or locate the note on the 5th string, then count over two strings and up two frets to find the same note one octave higher). Now play the root position chord, fingered as follows: third finger on 3rd string, second finger on 2nd string and first finger on 1st string.

Figure 13–7   3-2-1 string group minor chord inversions

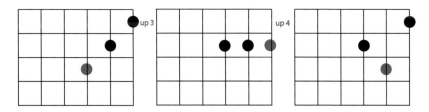

To play the first inversion minor chord, either locate the chord root on the 1st string and form the chord around that, or count up three frets on the 3rd string to the next voicing. Play the first inversion chord like this: either first, second, third or fourth finger barres all three notes.

The second inversion minor chord can be played either by finding the chord root on the 2nd string, or by counting up four frets on the 3rd string from the previous chord shape. Play this voicing as follows: second finger on 3rd string, third finger on 2nd string and first finger on 1st string.

As an example, to play an A minor chord using the above 3-2-1 string group voicings, the root position chord starts on either the 2nd or 14th fret of the 3rd string (note that if you play the chord on the 2nd fret, the chord shape changes as you remove your first finger to accommodate the open E string). The first inversion chord starts on the 5th fret of the 3rd string, and the second inversion chord starts on the 9th fret of the 3rd string.

How to Use and Practice Minor Chord Inversions

Since all of the previously illustrated voicings have the same notes as the open position and barre versions of the minor chord, you could theoretically insert any of them when a minor chord was required. This is where personal preference becomes your guide; some guitarists will elect to use these three-note chord shapes all the time, while others will use them more sparingly. To start using these new minor chord voicings to their fullest effect you'll need to spend a lot of time getting comfortable with them. One goal you can set for yourself is to be able to move smoothly from one chord to the next in a progression. This will often mean moving from a root position chord to a second or first inversion chord, a concept that can be difficult to master at first.

We'll use the classic Santana tune "Black Magic Woman" as a foundation for examining the basics of voice leading minor chords. Here's a chart of the chord progression. Each bar has four beats, and "min" is short for "minor."

D min / / /	D min / / /	A min / / /	A min / / /
D min / / /	D min / / /	G min / / /	G min / / /
D min / / /	A min / / /	D min / / /	D min / / /

Since the song has only three chords, D minor, A minor, and G minor, the process will remain fairly simple. We'll start by choosing a voicing for the D minor chord. This voicing will then dictate which voicings we play for both the A minor and G minor chords. This first example starts with a second inversion D minor chord voicing.

The second inversion D minor chord in **Figure 13–8** moves most smoothly to the root position A minor chord, as determined by the fact that the notes of the two voicings are as close together as possible while being played on the same string group. The D minor chord also moves most easily to the first inversion G minor chord.

Figure 13–8   D min / A min / G min on the 4-3-2 string group

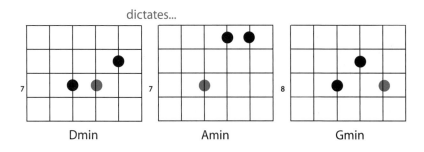

dictates...

Dmin   Amin   Gmin

Figure 13–9 starts on a first inversion D minor chord. This voicing moves most smoothly to a second inversion A minor chord, and a root position G minor chord. These are just several of the chord voicing possibilities you could use in playing "Black Magic Woman." I encourage you to experiment with others, making sure when you switch chords to move to the closest available voicing on the same string group.

Figure 13–9   D min / A min / G min on the 3-2-1 string group

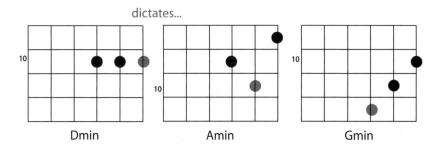

dictates...

Dmin   Amin   Gmin

The above exercise should not be considered a musical rule, however. I'm not saying you have to always move to the closest available voicing. But it does make good musical sense, and it's pleasing to the ear.

You also don't have to stay on one voicing for the duration of the chord. For example, you could play four different voicings for D minor in the first four bars of "Black Magic Woman" alone if you wanted to. The key is experimentation; in order to master these minor chord voicings, you'll need to play around with them extensively.

As far as how to practice minor chord inversions goes, here is a suggested practice regimen to help you learn these new minor chord shapes as quickly as possible.

Exercise 1

1. Randomly choose a minor chord to work with (such as A minor, or D minor, or Gb minor, etc.).
2. Start by playing just the root position chord on each of the four string groups.
3. Then play root position, first inversion, and second inversion chords on each of the four string groups.
4. If space allows, try playing the chords down the neck starting with root position. For example, play A minor on 5-4-3 string group in the root position at twelfth fret, then second inversion on seventh fret, then first inversion on fourth fret. Repeat on other string groups where possible).
5. Next, try picturing the root position chord shape on each string group, without playing it.
6. Then, play each first inversion shape.
7. Picture the root position and first inversion chord shapes on each string group, without playing them. Then play each second inversion shape.
8. Play the first inversion minor chord shapes on each of the four string groups, without playing the root position chord.
9. Repeat the above with second inversion chords.

Exercise 2

1. Randomly choose two minor chords.
2. Play the root position voicing of the first chord, then the root position voicing of the second chord. Repeat on each of the four string groups.
3. Play the root position voicing of the first chord, then the root position, first inversion and second inversion voicings for the second chord. Repeat on each string group. While you are playing the voicings for the second chord, remember where you played the root position voicing for the first chord.
4. Play the root position voicing for the first chord, then move directly to the closest voicing (on the same string group) for the second chord, whether it's the root position, first inversion, or second inversion. Repeat on each string group.
5. Play the first inversion voicing for the first chord, then move directly to the closest voicing (on the same string group) for the second chord, whether it's the root position, first inversion, or second inversion. Repeat on each string group.
6. Repeat the above beginning with the second inversion voicing, on each string group.
7. Play the lowest voicing available on a string group for the first chord (whether it's the root position, first or second inversion). Then move up the neck to the closest available inversion for the second chord. Move again up the neck to the next available inversion of the first chord. Repeat this process all the way up the neck, on each string group.

Exercise 3

1. Choose a song you know that includes only major and minor chords. If you're looking for a challenging suggestion, try playing the classic Jimi Hendrix song "Little Wing." Here's a chart of the chord progression. Each bar has four beats; "min" or "m" are short for "minor," and "maj" is short for "major." The 10th bar in the progression has two chord changes in it, each for two beats.

E min / / /	E min / / /	G maj / / /	G maj / / /
A min / / /	A min / / /	E min / / /	E min / / /
B min / / /	Bm / B♭ /	A min / / /	C maj / / /
G maj / / /	F maj / / /	C maj / / /	D maj / / /
D maj / / /	D maj / / /	D maj / / /	

2. Play each chord in the progression in root position, one string group at a time.
3. Play the root position of the first chord, then move to the closest inversion (on the same string group) of the second chord. Move again to the closest inversion of the third chord.
4. Repeat for as many chords as there are in the progression. Repeat on each string group. It might help to write down which voicings you used to keep track.
5. Try the above starting on the first inversion of the first chord. You should end up with an entirely new set of voicings for the same progression. Repeat on each string group.
6. Play the lowest voicing available on a string group for the first chord in the progression (whether it's the root position, first or second inversion). Move up the neck to the closest available inversion for the second chord. Move

again up the neck to the next available inversion of the third chord. Repeat this process all the way up the neck, on each string group.

7. Think of your own ideas for practicing these chord inversions.

By learning the inversions of major and minor chords, you've created almost limitless possibilities for yourself on the guitar.

Here's one example of these possibilities: It's an exercise for two guitarists, so grab a friend before you try it. Start by arpeggiating a G major chord voicing in root position on the 3-2-1 string group. Pick the chord as follows: 3rd string, 2nd string, 1st string, 2nd string. Repeat this pattern. Now, have your friend play the first inversion G major chord on the 3-2-1 string group. Have him or her play the exact same picking pattern as you, while you play the root position chord. Now you have an instant guitar harmony.

For a recorded example of this method, check out the solo at the end of the Eagles song "Hotel California." Try writing your own chord progression, and tackle this concept of using two guitar parts further.

This is just one of literally hundreds of different applications you'll be able to use chord inversions for. Take the time to learn them well, and your playing will improve dramatically. Have patience, and more importantly, have fun!

Advanced 2-Bar Strumming Pattern

Up until now, all the strumming patterns you've learned have been only one measure in length, with you simply repeating the 1-bar pattern. Now we'll look at a more complex two-measure strumming pattern.

This might be something of a challenge at first, but with practice you'll get the hang of it quickly.

Figure 13–10   2-bar strumming pattern

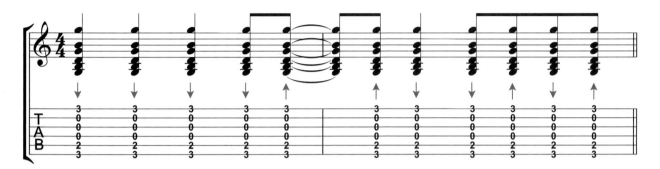

Figure 13–10 might look overwhelming on first sight, but (A) you don't have to read the standard notation, and (B) the chord on the tab is the same for the whole two bars, a G major. All you have to read is the arrow pattern, and if you use the constant down-up motion with your picking arm and only hit the indicated strums, this pattern should make sense.

You can listen to an MP3 file of this 2-bar strumming pattern on my About.com site: http://about.com/guitar/audiostrum2bar.

The key to learning a long strumming pattern is breaking down the strum, examining the smaller segments of the pattern, and then putting them back together. Let's look at the first six beats of the pattern, as shown in Figure 13–11.

By focusing on just this part of the strumming pattern at first, we'll make learning the whole strum much simpler. Be sure to keep your arm moving in a constant down-up motion, even when you're not actually strumming the strings. The pattern starts with down, down, down, down-up. Get comfortable playing this much of the pattern before continuing. Then add the final two strums (up-down). Now you're playing the pattern down, down, down, down-up, up-down. You can listen to an MP3 file of the first six

Figure 13–11   Incomplete strumming pattern

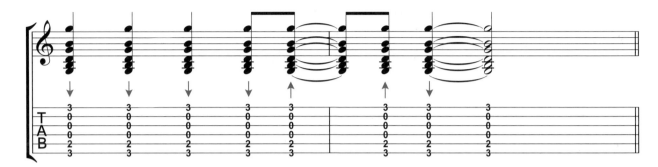

beats of this incomplete 2-bar strumming pattern on my About. com site: http://about.com/guitar/audiostrum2bar2.

Almost there! Now, we need to simply tack the last down-up-down-up to the end of the incomplete pattern and our full strumming pattern is complete—down, down, down, down-up, up-down, down-up-down-up.

Once you're able to play the strum once through, try repeating it four times in a row. And once you can do that, try switching to a different chord at the end of each 2-bar pattern. Note that the strum ends with an upstroke, and begins again immediately with a downstroke, so if there's a pause between repetitions of the pattern, you're not playing it correctly. If you're having trouble making the chord change quickly enough, it's okay to leave off the last upstroke of the strum to give yourself a little more time to move to the next chord.

Songs You Can Play Now

Take a stab at the following songs, and remember—push yourself! Try to play things that are difficult for you. Although challenging material may not be as much fun to play in the beginning, or sound

---

good when you first try it, you'll make big leaps forward in the long run by practicing it.

○ "I Will Survive," *Cake*
www.angelfire.com/band/frytabs/tabs/cake%5F%5F%5Fi%5Fwill%5Fsurvive.txt

○ "Kiss Me," *Sixpence None the Richer*
http://stringsnrythms.tripod.com/tab/english/group/html/group-sixpencenonethericher-kissme2.html

○ "The Wind Cries Mary," *Jimi Hendrix*
www.chordie.com/chord.pere/getsome.org/guitar/tabs/jimi_hendrix/TheWindCriesMary.chopro

As you move forward from here I hope you have a deep appreciation for the value of the time you spend practicing. All of the great guitarists we talk about in this book have one thing in common—they dedicated countless hours to the practice of their instrument and their music. It's not unusual for guitarists to spend five hours straight sitting at their music stands, studying whatever scale, riff, or song will take them to the next plateau. The reward of practicing is not only that your technique develops rapidly, but also that you have more and more fun as you go along—which is why the hours seem to fly by. So pick up your instrument, sit down, and take the next step on your journey.

1. Make sure your guitar is in tune.
2. Practice scales you've learned, using a metronome to keep time. Try palm muting the scale. Try sliding from note to note. Try hammering on as you ascend the scale, and pulling off as you descend.

►►►
The strumming pattern that we studied in this chapter will work well for "I Will Survive" and for "Kiss Me." On "I Will Survive," play the strumming pattern once for each chord (and twice for the last two bars of E major). The chords for "The Wind Cries Mary" are ones that you know now. If you'd like to learn more about the classic riff that this song is built around, you can check out the tutorial on my site: http://about.com/guitar/featuredlick.

3. Practice your major seventh chords. Pick a random note (such as Ab) and try playing that note's major seventh chord on both the sixth string (fourth fret) and the fifth string (eleventh fret).
4. Practice all of your seventh chords. These are our newest chord shapes, so it will assuredly take a while for you to absorb them. Try playing some or all of the following chord progressions. Choose any strumming pattern you feel comfortable with. Try these progressions:

Bb major 7–G minor 7–C minor 7–F7
D minor 7–G minor 7–Bb7–A7
C7–F7–C7–G7

Try playing these chords in a variety of different ways—all on sixth string, all on fifth string, and a combination of both. There are a large number of possible ways to play each of these chord progressions. You can also try making up your own chord progressions with seventh chords. Don't be afraid to experiment!
5. Practice this chapter's minor chord inversions on all four string groups.
6. Do some string bending. Do this often, because you won't get better at it until you build up some finger strength. Even if it's not fun for you now, try doing it for one or two minutes every time you play guitar. You'll be happy you did.
7. Keep practicing the fingerpicking patterns from Chapters 9 and 10.
8. Try to play all of the songs listed in this chapter, and keep playing those from previous lessons.

This is the last lesson chapter in the book. I'm sure you feel ready to go charging ahead and learn more! Remember—chances are good that there are areas of the previous lessons you've neglected or forgotten, so I urge you to go back to the beginning and see if you can work your way through all of the lesson chapters, memorizing and practicing everything.

Thanks for all of your hard work. You've come a long way since the day we studied how to hold a pick and what a fingerboard is! That day must seem light years behind you now. The beauty of playing guitar is that there's always more to learn, more to explore. Each new technique you learn builds on all the others you know and takes you farther down the path to guitar mastery.

Get Linked

*You can find information about subjects above and beyond what we've had time to discuss in these chapters on my **About.com** site. Since we've been discussing a Jimi Hendrix riff in the songs we're working on in this chapter, I thought you might like to explore more of the work of this guitar genius on this extensive tab archive. Check out this interesting link.*

**JIMI HENDRIX
GUITAR TABLATURE**

Archive of Jimi Hendrix guitar tab
http://about.com/guitar/hendrixtab

Chapter 14

Taking Care of and Maintaining Your Instrument

Changing Strings

The strings are the voice of your guitar, the source from which all the notes you play are generated, so they're deserving of your attention. As a guitarist you'll need to know all about strings, including how to change them, which brands and types of strings you prefer, and how many extras you need to have at all times.

Take a look at the strings of your acoustic guitar. What sort of shape are they in? Are they discolored? Maybe even rusty? Is there visible dirt between the windings of the wound strings? Do the second and first strings feel as if they're coated with crud? If you answered "yes" to any of these questions, or if it's been several months since you put new strings on your guitar, you're ready for a string change!

How often should I change my strings?

▶ When I'm playing my acoustic guitar a lot, I change the strings at least every two weeks, and even more than that if I'm using it for gigs. It's probably not necessary for you to be quite as diligent with keeping new strings on your guitar in the beginning, but once you're playing regularly, changing strings a minimum of every couple of months is a very good idea.

Just like brake pads on a car, guitar strings wear out with use. Old guitar strings behave badly, losing their tuning more quickly, sounding dull, and giving you problems with intonation. Old guitar strings also break, often at the most inopportune moment.

New strings make your guitar sound brighter and more alive, produce more overtones, and generally make the instrument easier to play. They take a little time to stretch out when you first change them before they'll stay in tune, but after a few minutes of stretching and retuning they'll stabilize, and then your guitar will sound the best it can.

You should always have, at a minimum, one complete set of extra strings in your guitar case at all times. Most guitarists carry two or three complete sets in their cases, as well as extra "singles" of the strings most likely to break, those being the third, second, and first strings because they're thinner.

Be sure to head into any live playing situation with new strings on your guitar, and several more sets of strings packed in your case, should you break a string during your performance.

By now you're probably wondering what kind of strings you should buy. There is no single answer to this question, because every guitar player has an opinion about which strings are best. Let's put aside any discussion of guitar-string manufacturers for a moment and just discuss the type of strings needed for your guitar. Because you're playing acoustic guitar, you need—you guessed it—acoustic guitar strings. If your instrument is a classical guitar, you need classical guitar strings or nylon strings.

You also need to consider the gauge (thickness) of strings you want. This is where personal preference comes into play. I recommend starting out with medium-gauge strings, and varying from that as your preference develops. An oversimplified rule of thumb is that thicker strings provide better tone, but are harder to play.

If you're intimidated by the thought of buying a set of strings from a guitar store, don't be. Simply march in, and say "I'd like a set of (insert the brand name, such as D'Addario, Fender, or Dean Markley) medium-gauge acoustic guitar strings please." Prices vary from store to store, but a basic set of acoustic strings shouldn't set you back more than $8.

To learn more about the different brands of strings that are available, check out the guitar-string manufacturers resource on my About.com site. You'll find the link in the Get Linked section at the end of this chapter.

Now we'll explore the process of changing the strings on your guitar.

Begin by finding a flat surface on which to lay the guitar. A table works well, but the floor also works in a pinch. Lay a towel on the surface to cushion your guitar. Position yourself in front of the instrument, with the guitar's sixth string closest to you. Completely loosen the sixth string of the guitar first by turning the tuner. If you're unsure of which direction to turn the tuner to loosen the string, pluck the string before you begin turning the tuner. The pitch of the note will get lower as you loosen the string.

Once the string has been completely loosened, uncoil it from the tuning peg at the head of the guitar. Then remove the other end of the string from the bridge by removing the sixth-string bridge pin from the bridge of the guitar (see **Figure 14–1**). Commonly, bridge pins will provide some resistance when you're trying to remove them. If this is the case, use a pair of pliers to gently coax the bridge pin out of the bridge.

Discard the old string. Using a soft cloth, wipe down any areas of the guitar you aren't able to reach when the sixth string is on the instrument. Use a separate cloth or paper towel to clean the residue off of the fingerboard underneath the sixth string. If you have guitar polish, now is the time to use it on the guitar body.

Figure 14–1   Bridge pin

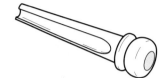

While some guitarists remove all strings from their guitar at once and then replace all of them, I highly advise against this procedure. The six tuned strings of a guitar produce a great deal of tension on the neck of the instrument, which is a good thing. Removing all six strings at once drastically changes this tension, which many guitar necks don't react to very well. Sometimes, when all six strings are replaced at once, the strings will sit impossibly high off the fingerboard. *Change your strings one at a time to avoid these issues.*

Uncoil your brand-new sixth string from its package. Note that there is a small ball on one end of the string. Slide the ball end of the string down a couple of inches into the hole in the bridge. Now, replace the bridge pin back into the hole, aligning the carved slot of the pin with the string (see **Figure 14–2**).

Figure 14–2   Sixth string being inserted into hole in bridge, with pin

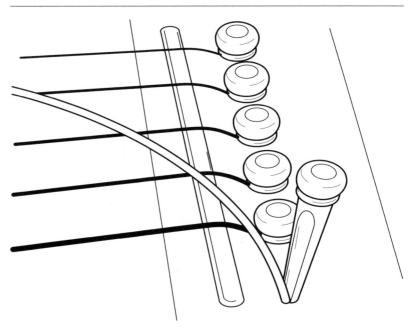

As you replace the bridge pin, lightly pull on the string (being careful not to crimp the string with your fingers), until you feel the ball slip into place. If the pin pops back out when you very lightly pull on the string, repeat the process and use your thumb to firmly press the bridge pin down. This may take a bit of practice, but you'll get a feel for it quickly. Don't use any tool to hammer the bridge pin in—this can cause the wood of the bridge to split.

Now, very gently pull the string up toward the headstock of the guitar, applying just enough force so that most of the visible slack disappears from the string. Pull the string about one generous inch past the tuning peg you will be feeding it through, and, using your fingers, crimp the string to a 90-degree angle so the end of the string points in the direction of the tuning peg (see **Figure 14–3**).

Figure 14–3 Headstock with string at correct length and bent 90 degrees

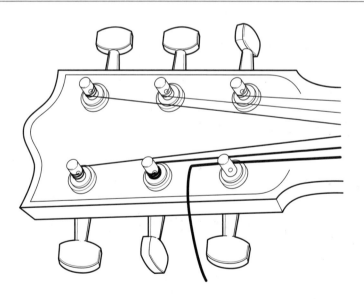

▶ There are several tools for changing strings that you should keep in your guitar case: wire cutters to cut your old strings for removal, and to cut the ends off of your new strings once they're on; pliers to help lift up stubborn bridge pins; and a soft cloth to wipe down the guitar. Guitar polish is optional, but if you want to polish your instrument, the best time to get under the string area is during string changes. A string winder also is optional, but it will save the wrist of your fretting hand by allowing you to crank the string quickly onto the tuning post.

Without yet feeding the string through the tuning peg, turn the tuner until the hole in the tuning peg will allow the crimped end of the string to slide straight through it.

Slide the string through the tuning peg until you hit the crimp in the string. At this point, you may again crimp the end of the string that's protruding from the tuning peg, in order to help keep the string in place as you tighten it (see **Figure 14–4**).

Figure 14–4   Sixth string crimped through tuning post

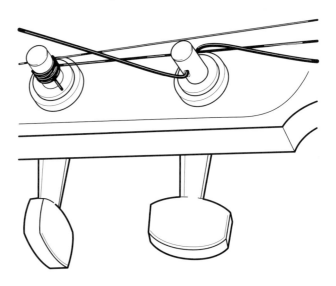

Now, we'll begin tightening the string, to slowly bring it into tune. If you own a string winder (see **Figure 14–5**), it will come in handy now.

If you don't have a winder, consider purchasing one—it can be a big timesaver while changing strings, and will only set you back a couple of dollars.

Figure 14-5   String winder

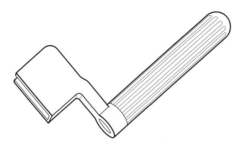

Begin turning the tuning peg slowly and evenly in a counterclockwise manner. To help keep the excess slack in the string from acting erratically while you rotate the tuner, use the hand not tuning the guitar to create artificial tension in the string. Gently press the sixth string against the fingerboard with your index finger, using the rest of your fingers to lightly pull up on the string (see **Figure 14-6**). Meanwhile, keep rotating the tuner with the other hand. Mastering this technique will save you a great deal of hassle when changing strings.

Figure 14-6   The picking hand creating tension on the string

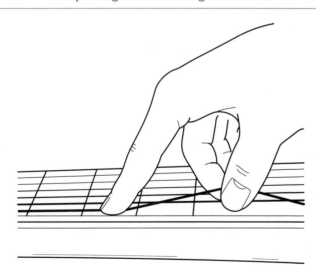

As you begin to rotate the tuner, watch to make sure the wrapped string passes over the end portion of the string that's protruding from the end of the tuning peg, on the first wraparound (see **Figure 14–7**).

Figure 14–7   First rotation string wind, over top of string end

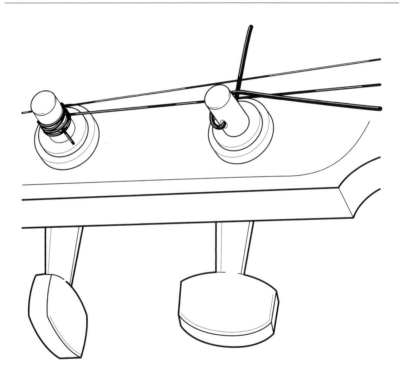

Note that it's normal for the bridge pin to pop up slightly while you're tightening the string. Use your thumb to push it back down into position.

Immediately after the wrapped string has passed over the string end, guide the string so that on the next pass, it will wrap under the string end. All subsequent wraparounds will also wrap under the string end, each wrap going below the last. Avoid having strings physically lying on top of, or crossing over, one another. Keep turning the tuner counterclockwise, until the string has been brought approximately into tune. At this point, your tuning peg should look approximately like the one in **Figure 14–8** (there may be additional string wraps on the peg if you left more slack in the string initially).

Figure 14–8   Remaining rotations of string wind below string end

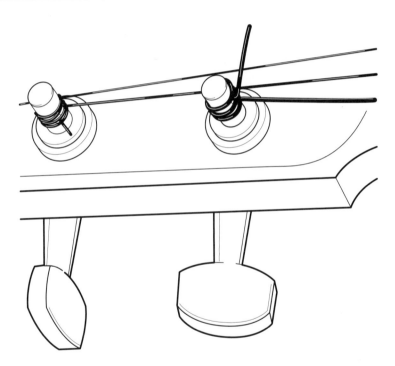

Although the string has now been brought into approximate tune, you'll find that the tuning will be hard to maintain unless you take a moment to stretch out the string. Grab the string somewhere over the sound hole, and gently pull it upward for several seconds to stretch it (see **Figure 14–9** on the following page).

Figure 14–9   Pulling string to stretch it

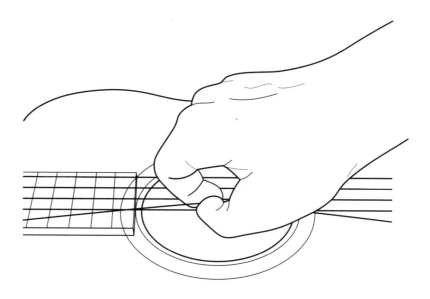

Now check the tuning. You'll probably find that the string has gone somewhat out of tune. Retune the string, and repeat this process. Do this several times, until the string no longer goes out of tune (or until the tuning changes only slightly).

Finally, use wire cutters (or the equivalent) to trim the excess string. Simply take your cutters and snip off the end of the string protruding from the tuning peg. Try to leave about ¼" of string remaining. Congratulations—you've just changed the sixth string of your guitar. It may have taken you a while, but with practice, the process will go much more quickly.

If you managed to change your sixth string, then the other five strings will only get easier, as you continue to gain experience. The only part of the process that will differ as you continue to change the remaining strings is the direction you'll feed the strings through the tuning pegs for strings three, two, and one (see **Figure 14–10**).

Because the tuners for these three strings are on the other side of the headstock, they'll need to be fed through the tuning pegs in the opposite direction as strings six, five, and four.

Figure 14–10   Headstock with correct string entry directions

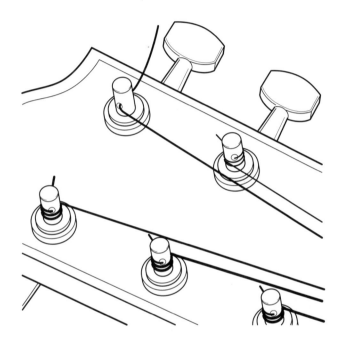

Because of this, the direction you'll turn the tuners to tighten the strings is also opposite. While holding the guitar in normal playing position, turning the tuners "up" (away from the body of the guitar) will tune the string higher for strings six, five, and four. In order to tune strings three, two, and one higher, you'll need to turn the tuners for those strings "down" (toward the body of the guitar).

Note that if you own a guitar that has all six tuners on the same side of the headstock, you'll ignore this and put on all six strings in the exact same manner.

That's it! You've learned the process of restringing and tuning an acoustic guitar. It may seem tricky at first, but after a few full string changes, you'll have the procedure mastered.

Traveling with Your Guitar

Your guitar is a delicate instrument that needs your tender loving care and protection. The more you play, the more you'll want your guitar with you wherever you go, and this will naturally lead to traveling with your guitar. While taking your instrument with you on trips can be a rewarding experience, it also exposes your guitar to many dangerous situations.

Among the worst of these are the dangers posed by air travel, especially if your instrument is placed into the baggage compartment. Extreme shifts in temperature and humidity take place in the baggage compartment during a flight, and these are two factors that the delicate wood of your guitar is especially sensitive to. Because of this, musicians have gone to great lengths since the dawn of air travel to keep their instruments out of the baggage compartment.

There's a story about the great cellist Yo-Yo Ma carrying his cello—which is bigger than a guitar—down the jetway to the door of an airplane. The flight attendant blocks his way with her hand outstretched. "Whoa whoa whoa there, sir!" she says. "What is that you're carrying?" "This?" asks the musician, holding up the large hardshell cello case. "This is an oboe." The flight attendant checks her list of acceptable instruments to carry on board, spots "oboe" on it—and waves him on by.

If only it were that easy nowadays. Airplanes used to come with coat closets and extra space in the galleys where you could usually convince a flight attendant to place your guitar, but no more. These days those extra spaces are gone, flights are full, and a guitar case is way bigger than the allowable carryon limit. Translation—your instrument is going into baggage.

To minimize the risk, be sure to take the following precautions:

- Loosen the strings of your guitar about a whole step before putting it on a plane. The variations in temperature in the baggage compartment cause normally tense strings to get much tighter, which puts too much pressure on the neck of the instrument. This can cause a few different types of spectacular damage.
- Use only a solid hardshell case for plane travel. Cardboard cases or soft gig bags will not cut it in a baggage compartment.
- Make sure your guitar is snug in its case—it shouldn't move around. If there's any extra space in there, fill it up with a towel or some other soft protective material.
- If possible, carry your guitar all the way to your boarding gate and ask the airline staff to hand-carry it onto the plane. When you arrive at your destination gate, ask the airline staff there if they can retrieve your instrument by hand and bring it to you at the gate.

Automobile travel presents its own set of risks. In this case your primary enemy is the trunk of the car, where temperatures become extremely cold in the winter and extremely hot in the summer. If space permits, always put your guitar in the back seat, where a more even temperature is maintained. When you get out of the car, take your instrument with you, because the interior of the car also reaches extreme temperatures quickly during summer and winter.

Cleaning and Polishing Your Guitar

The most important part of keeping your guitar clean is in the way you approach it every day. The great majority of the dirt that gets on your guitar comes from your own hands, which leave a mix of dirt and the oil from your skin anywhere you touch it.

It's a great idea to wash your hands every time before you pick up your instrument. Once you've done that, use a clean towel or cloth to wipe down the back of the neck of your guitar, as well as the strings and fingerboard. Playing a clean instrument with clean hands feels good, and it makes moving around the neck much smoother.

By the same token, when you're done playing your guitar, take the clean cloth and wipe down the back of the neck, the fingerboard, the entire length of the strings, and every surface of the body of the instrument before you put it away. Taking these simple steps will preserve the finish on your guitar and extend the life of your strings.

Occasionally your guitar will require a complete cleaning to keep every surface in tiptop shape. You'll want to have a few tools on hand for cleaning your instrument:

- Two soft cotton cloths, one to dampen and the other to be left dry
- A small 1"-wide soft-bristled paintbrush
- Some very fine (0000 gauge) steel wool
- Guitar polish or surface cleaner, if desired

A lot of the dirt, smudges, and fingerprints that accumulate on your guitar can be easily removed by wiping the area with a cotton cloth slightly dampened with water, and then drying it immediately with a clean, dry cloth, also cotton.

Use the paintbrush to remove dust from hard-to-reach areas, such as underneath the strings on the top of the guitar, and the front of the headstock under the strings.

To clean the strings, grasp them inside a dry cloth held between your thumb and first finger and run the cloth up and down the length. You'll see quite a bit of dirt come off on the cloth.

Cleaning the fingerboard and frets is best done while changing strings, but here's the process: First, using a damp cotton cloth, rub the fingerboard between the frets to remove the buildup of dirt and oil. In most cases, especially if you do it frequently, this will be all it takes to get the fingerboard clean. If you're faced with stubborn buildup, use the fine steel wool to remove it—so long as your fingerboard is made of unfinished wood, such as ebony or rosewood. The steel wool will also shine up your frets. Rub it across the fingerboard in the same direction as the frets are laid. Caution: If your fingerboard has a glossy finish, steel wool will degrade it. If water isn't enough to clean it, you can try a little guitar polish on a cloth.

If you've cleaned the body of your guitar with water and it's still showing imperfections, you might want to use guitar polish or another form of surface cleaner to clean and polish the surface further. Guitars come in many different finishes, which require different kinds of care. If your guitar has a glossy finish you can use a fine guitar polish, such as the one made by Martin guitars, to remove minor scratches and give the wood an even shine. If your guitar has a natural or satin finish, however, this kind of guitar polish will damage the intended finish, so it's best to stick to water using the damp-and-dry-cloths technique. If that's not enough, you can use a mild soap-and-water solution, rinsed with pure water on a damp cotton cloth and dried immediately with a dry cloth.

General Guitar Protection

Even when it's just sitting unused at home, your guitar needs attention to stay in top condition. Here's how to protect your instrument from common dangers that threaten it.

Extremes in temperature and humidity play as much of a role in your guitar's condition at home as they do when you travel, so it's worth our time to look more closely at how to guard against the damage they can cause.

TOOLS YOU NEED

▶ How can you tell what the humidity level is? To find out you need a handy tool called a hygrometer, which measures humidity. Radio Shack makes a cool little unit called the Indoor/Outdoor Thermometer with Hygrometer (model #63-1032) that combines a hygrometer with a thermometer in one compact digital unit for about $25. This unit will monitor both of the critical conditions your guitar is exposed to inside your home—or even inside your guitar case.

Don't store your instrument close to a heater or an air conditioner, or anyplace where temperatures vary much from the mid-70s (Fahrenheit). High temperatures, especially if accompanied by high humidity, can adversely affect the glue that holds your guitar together; for example, the seams may split.

If you move your guitar from one extreme temperature to another, such as bringing it indoors on a cold winter day, let it stay in its case for a while as the case gradually warms up before you open the case and expose your instrument to the indoor air. Sudden changes in temperature can cause cracks in the finish of your guitar.

Extremes in humidity cause the wood of your instrument to expand and contract in bad ways, so it's good to know the general humidity of your home. The ideal humidity for guitars is about 50 percent. If your home humidity level is more than 10 percent in either direction, you might consider getting a humidifier, or a dehumidifier, to move it in the right direction.

Storing your guitar in its case when you're not playing it is by far the safest approach to keeping it in good condition. I know we've talked about the advantages of leaving your instrument setting out on a guitar stand in terms of making it easy to start practicing, and those still hold true. The compromise might be to take your instrument out and put it on the stand when the playing part of your day begins, leaving it out until you're ready to go to bed. At that time, put it back in its case.

Keeping Your Action Correct

Action is a term used to describe the height of the strings above the fingerboard and frets. The height of the action makes a big difference in how playable your instrument will be. If the action is too high, meaning the strings are too far away from the fingerboard, it will be a struggle to press down the strings to play clean-sounding chords and single-note melodies, especially as you move higher up on the neck. On the other hand, if the action is too low, the strings will buzz against the frets when you play and produce sounds you don't want.

Most guitarists want to have the lowest action possible without having any fret buzz, which is the setting that makes the instrument easiest to play. However, some players like the action to be higher so they can hit the strings harder without fret buzz, and play louder. Higher action is also better for playing slide guitar.

The height of the action is determined by three factors—the height of the bridge, the height of the nut, and the way the truss rod is adjusted. None of these are things you should try to adjust yourself unless you know what you're doing, because chances are you'll do something that damages your instrument. It's common, for example, for people to think they can lower the action just by adjusting the truss rod, but this would be a mistake. The truss rod is for adjusting the "bow" of the neck, meaning how much the strings are pulling the neck forward. The truss rod will lower the action, but the amount of tightening it would require might put too much stress on the rod. Usually the first adjustment that's made to lower the action of an acoustic guitar is to lower the saddle of the bridge.

If you think your action needs to be adjusted, take your guitar into a music store and have a guitar repairperson check it out and make the proper adjustments. Ask for an estimate first, and make sure it's within your budget before any actual work begins.

When to See the Repair Guy

As long as we're on the subject of taking your instrument in, when is it necessary to take your guitar in to the repair guy or gal? The most common reason is to have the guitar "set up" once in a while, meaning having the string heights adjusted at the bridge and

How much should I be spending on guitar repairs?

▶ Guitar repairs can be expensive, and you have to weigh that cost against the value of your instrument, both financially and sentimentally. If your guitar cost you $300 initially, you'd want to think twice before spending $200 to repair it. But if it cost $300 initially and you've been playing it for ten years and love it, that could be another matter. I'd say that if you've been playing an inexpensive guitar that you bought as a beginner and that instrument needs serious structural repair, it's time to cut your losses and start over with a new—and ideally, better—instrument.

nut, along with a truss rod adjustment or neck angle adjustment if required, to make the action perfect. Other reasons for taking your instrument into the shop would include the occurrence of structural problems, such as seams separating, cracks in the wood, severe warping, and breakage.

One other maintenance issue we haven't discussed is the occasional need to have your guitar refretted. Frets wear out over time because strings are constantly being pressed and rubbed against them. How long this takes depends on the gauge of strings you use and how hard you play. If you notice any imperfections in your frets, such as depressions and other misshaping, it's time to have your frets replaced.

The other reason for seeing the repair guy or gal is if you want modifications made in your instrument, such as adding a second strap button if your guitar didn't come with one, or replacing inexpensive tuners with a better, smoother set. These operations are best done by the professionals, especially if you have no experience at it.

Get Linked

*You can find more information on the subjects we've discussed in this chapter on my **About.com** site. Check out these helpful links.*

GUITAR-STRING RESOURCES

Guitar-string resources, including discount online vendors, string manufacturer Web sites, and more

 http://about.com/guitar/stringresources

GUITAR REPAIR RESOURCES

Online resource for extensive information about guitar diagnostics and repair

 http://about.com/guitar/repairresources

Chapter 15

Where Do You Go from Here?

Acoustic Guitarists Who Changed the World

Musical-instrument museums are full of instruments whose lifespan was little more than decades. The guitar, on the other hand, first appeared in the fifteenth century. More than five hundred years later, it has become one of the most popular instruments on earth, due in no small part to the talent and dedication that guitarists brought to the instrument.

What follows is a sampling of guitarists who changed the musical world and led the way for the guitar's acceptance as a serious and enduring instrument. This is by no means a complete list—it simply highlights a few of the guitar luminaries who have preceded us.

Andrés Segovia

As far as classical guitar is concerned, Segovia was The Man. By transcribing important composers' music for the guitar for the first time and then playing it with unprecedented technique and passion, the Spanish virtuoso elevated the guitar from an instrument relegated to playing in taverns to an instrument finally respected in the classical music community.

Robert Johnson

Although he was not the originator of the Delta blues, Robert Johnson is considered the king of the genre, and his songs have been recorded by many top rock players from the 1960s to this day. According to blues legend, Johnson met the devil at a crossroads in Mississippi and sold his soul for the ability to play well. Before you try doing the same, note that his recording career lasted only three years before he died.

Django Reinhardt

In the 1930s and '40s, Django, along with his partner violinist Stephane Grappelli, burned up the stages in Paris with a frenetic form of hot jazz that had never been heard before. Many guitarists have pored over Django's recordings trying to figure out his technique—a task that becomes all the more frustrating when you realize that he did it all with only three working fingers on his fretting hand!

John Fahey

This American guitarist broke new ground in the areas of fingerpicking and open tunings. His most famous recording, a series of requiems of his own composition released in 1967, presents long explorations of tonality and rhythm that grow and develop organically with the beauty of a kaleidoscope. Fahey and his guitar style created the foundation of the American Primitive Guitar school of music, which draws on the blues and a wide variety of other American musical influences for inspiration.

Michael Hedges

The first two albums by this breakthrough artist in the late 1980s and early '90s took acoustic guitar playing in a new direction. Hedges had great compositional talent and fingerpicking technique, to which he added his own system of right-hand tapping and other percussive effects to draw previously unheard sounds from the instrument.

Today's Top Players on Acoustic

What follows is a sampling of the guitarists who are playing today and who are stretching the boundaries of the instrument with their talent and imagination.

Again, this list is by no means complete, but simply highlights a few of the guitar players who were important in the twentieth century and/or are now leading players who are taking the instrument into the twenty-first century.

Julian Bream

This British guitarist has done more than anyone to propel twentieth-century classical guitar music forward. His playing is flawless and transcendent, and he is considered one of the leading classical guitarists in the world.

Joni Mitchell

This Canadian guitarist, singer, and songwriter is highly regarded for her excellent fingerpicking technique as well as for her ceaseless exploration of open tunings. She has set new standards in the areas of folk, jazz, and pop music, and her songs have been covered by many other influential bands over the years.

Jorma Kaukonen

Even though he's most famous as lead electric guitarist for Jefferson Airplane, Kaukonen began as an acoustic guitarist and has always been a proponent of acoustic guitar music. His performances of twentieth-century American blues and folk songs throughout the years reintroduced them to new, younger audiences. You can study with him today at his Fur Peace Ranch guitar camp in Ohio.

Leo Kottke

This fingerpicking wizard burst onto the scene in 1969 with an album of instrumental guitar music in the school of the American Primitive Guitar movement (in fact, the album was released by John Fahey's record label). Kottke was greatly influenced by Fahey, and the two have recorded and performed together over the years.

Bill Connors

This brilliant jazz guitarist rocketed to fame as the first electric guitarist in Chick Corea's seminal band Return to Forever. When he dropped out of that band after one album, he switched over to acoustic guitar and made several excellent acoustic albums for the ECM label.

Badi Assad

This Brazilian classical guitarist is a fiery talent with magnificent technique and passion. She plays Brazilian classics as well as her own compositions and is widely considered of the best fingerstyle artists playing today. She has collaborated with some of the top jazz guitarists, including Pat Metheny, Larry Coryell, and John Abercrombie.

Al DiMeola
Possibly the land speed record holder for fastest single-note melodies, DiMeola shines on both acoustic and electric guitars. He is a master technician who has explored jazz, classical, and flamenco guitar and has recorded great examples of each genre. He is so fast he sometimes has to use palm muting to make sure his audience can differentiate the notes in his phrases as they go by at Mach 3.

John Williams
This Australian guitarist is regarded as one of the top classical guitarists playing today. He was a pupil of Segovia, and has worked extensively with Julian Bream as well as collaborating with many of the leading musicians of the day in many different musical genres.

Pat Metheny
Generally found residing at the top of best artist polls, this popular guitarist is always pushing the limits of whatever guitar or musical genre he's involved with. His approach blends elements of traditional American blues, folk, and pop guitar into his distinctive jazz guitar style.

John McLaughlin
Best known for playing electric guitar with Miles Davis and in his own Mahavishnu Orchestra, British jazz guitarist McLaughlin took the acoustic guitar path after these two stints, recording impressive and technique-laden acoustic albums both as a solo artist and with his acoustic group Shakti, as well as recording trio albums with guitarists Al DiMeola and Paco de Lucia.

Alex DeGrassi

Another proponent of the open tuning and the dazzling fingerpicking style, DeGrassi shines in the solo acoustic guitar format. The influence of John Fahey and Leo Kottke is apparent in his approach to the instrument, but his style also incorporates Latin, jazz, and world beat idioms into a unique sound.

Doc Watson

Known for his clean, crisp flatpicking style, this innovative guitarist helped redefine the role of the guitar as a solo instrument in bluegrass music when he started playing fast, complicated fiddle parts on the guitar. Watson paved the way for the wave of flatpicking bluegrass guitarists that followed, including luminaries Ricky Skaggs and Tony Rice.

Kaki King

Taking solo acoustic guitar in new directions, Kaki King uses both hands to attack her instrument percussively in a variety of ways, including thumping the body, slapping the strings, fingerpicking with dexterity, strumming, hammer-ons, and two-handed tapping to create textural compositions that take fingerstyle guitar into the twenty-first century.

Ani DiFranco

This dynamic performer combines excellent fingerpicking with open tunings to create original compositions in the folk-rock idiom. Her guitar style is rhythmic and dynamic and full of surprise twists, turns, stops, and accents that punctuate her vocals.

D'Gary

A guitar wizard from Madagascar and a pioneer in the creation and use of open tunings, D'Gary mesmerizes audiences with his powerful fingerpicking style, which is syncopated in rhythms and phrases that intertwine in a fascinating and unpredictable way. His is an outstanding, original voice on acoustic guitar.

Careers in Guitar

If you have a consuming interest in music and the guitar, I'm sure the thought of becoming a professional musician has crossed your mind. If you think a career in music is for you and you can't already read music (meaning standard notation as opposed to tab) I recommend that you start learning now. As mentioned earlier, there are many professional performing musicians who don't read music, but if you elect not to learn, there will be many doors in the music business that will be closed to you. We'll talk more about reading in a minute.

The following are a few of the careers you could pursue as a guitarist. These are not mutually exclusive—most musicians move back and forth between two or more of these roles in their musical lives.

Performing artist Being a performing artist offers the most direct interaction with your audience. The flow of energy between the performer and the audience can be exhilarating. When the members of the audience are obvious in their appreciation, and showing their support, it spurs the performing artist on to new heights, which thrills the audience even more. This cycle is immensely rewarding for everyone involved.

Recording artist Recording in the studio gives a musician the opportunity to create a "perfect" version of the piece being recorded. During live performances there often are details in the playing or in the way the sound is being mixed in the room that could be better—but there are no second chances. In the recording studio, attention is paid to every minute detail in a way

ELSEWHERE ON THE WEB

▶ To read more about the many careers that are possible in music, check out this area of the Berklee School of Music Web site: www .berklee.edu/careers. The site goes into detail about a wide array of careers. Beyond performing, recording, and composing, there are a hundred other possibilities you may never have thought of.

that's impossible in live performance. The tonal quality of every instrument is carefully tailored before, during, and after a piece is recorded, and any mistakes that may occur in the playing itself can be **punched in**, or corrected. During the **mixing** process all of the instruments are blended together so that their relationship to each other is ideal. And in the **mastering** process the overall sound of the piece is polished. The result is a recording that presents your music in its best possible light.

Studio musician The difference between being a recording artist and a studio musician is that a studio musician has to be able to arrive at a recording session and immediately become part of the producer's vision of the piece being recorded. This requires a broad knowledge of musical styles, the ability to sight-read music and play it instantly, and the ability to change your approach to the music being played on a dime if asked to by the producer.

Composer / songwriter Many performing and recording artists are also songwriters or composers who create the music that they play. Writing your own music gives you the opportunity to express your thoughts and emotions in a different and more personal way than by playing interpretations of other peoples' music. By listening as widely as possible to the music of the past and present and pulling out the components of that music that are most appealing, the composer develops his or her own unique set of influences, which become the composer's "voice." Some songwriters and composers write music exclusively for other people to perform, either as freelancers or in staff positions at record companies or music publishing houses.

Teacher Teaching is another career in music that can be tremendously rewarding. This involves instructing students, either individually or in classes, on guitar technique and (usually) on reading guitar tab and standard notation. There are many settings in which you might teach, from being a private instructor to teaching in school or even teaching on TV or making instructional DVDs. It's wonderful to watch the beautiful process as a student improves and gets excited about guitar under your tutelage.

Ready to Read?

There comes a point in your development as a guitarist when you must decide if you're interested in learning guitar in a deep and comprehensive way. If the answer is "yes," then learning the basics of sight-reading is essential.

In these chapters I've tried to keep the lessons as much "fun" as possible, meaning that they're free from excessive technical exercises, music theory, and sight-reading. But the truth is, if you want to become a real musician, these all are important areas to explore.

In a perfect world I'd be able to provide you with a great online resource for learning to sight-read music on the guitar, but the topic is just too broad in scope to be handled well online. Currently there are no resources on the Web that do a good job of teaching guitarists to read music, in my opinion, so I'm going to recommend a purchase to you—the excellent Modern Method for Guitar books, by William G. Leavitt.

Often referred to as "the Berklee books," this series of inexpensive (usually under $15) publications is a valuable resource for working on sight-reading, and honing your technical skills on the guitar. Leavitt does not hold your hand through the learning process, but with some focused practice you'll learn to read music and improve your technique through playing some of the etudes (pieces of music written to teach particular skills) presented in the book.

TOOLS YOU NEED

▶ If you're interested in reviewing the vast number of guitar books and DVDs that are out there in order to find the ones that are right for you, visit the larger music store Web sites, which maintain the most comprehensive lists of resources. One place to start would be the Sam Ash book and DVD location. When you get there, click on "Instructional: guitar." Just go to www.samash.com/depart ment/booksvideo.

You can spend a great deal of time with these books (there are three in the series), as there is a ton of information contained within the pages of each one. If you're serious about becoming a "musician," rather than someone who just strums a guitar at parties (not that there is anything wrong with that), I highly recommend that you pick up at least one of these publications.

Where to Continue Your Study

Even though we have made a great deal of progress and you've learned a lot in the chapters of this book, we've barely scratched the surface of all there is to know about music theory, harmony, composition, and guitar technique. The body of knowledge is limitless as well as constantly growing, as musicians continue to push the envelope of what is possible. The more you learn, the more you realize how much there is still left to learn. That's the journey we've embarked on. Fortunately, the process is incredibly fun and rewarding—especially when you suddenly wake up with the ability to play something that you've struggled with and felt was impossible for weeks—and the thrill and energy from those leaps in ability will fuel your desire to continue. So, keep going!

There are several avenues available to you for continuing your study of music and the guitar. Most guitarists use many of these avenues of study at one time or another as they build their musicianship. Think of them as opportunities that are available to you should you want to pursue them. The more serious you become about playing guitar, the more of your time, energy, and resources you'll be willing to invest.

For some people, self-directed study of the guitar works best. This approach gives you the ability to change direction spontaneously, investigating and practicing whatever most appeals to you at the moment. It definitely requires a lot of motivation and dedication, as you're the only one who determines how hard you work at it.

Be a bookworm. There are books available about every aspect of learning guitar, including books of chords and chord progressions, books of songs, books on sight-reading, music theory, harmony, composition, and books on any style of music in particular that you might want to pursue. Studying from books has the advantage that you can move at your own pace through the material, and it's all available for review at any time. I recommend that you get at least one comprehensive chord book for information and reference.

DVDs are a great resource. Studying with DVDs has all the advantages of books with one critical addition—you get to see all the techniques you're trying to learn, performed right in front of you, and you can rewind as many times as you like while you absorb them. Additionally, you get the opportunity to study with musicians you might never get to meet otherwise, possibly including the guitarists you most admire.

Take a class. Some schools and music stores offer guitar classes in which groups of students of approximately the same skill level come together with a teacher. The advantage to this approach is that you get to interact with the teacher and ask questions during the class. The teacher can also assess your individual level and offer instruction and advice based on your own needs.

Get a private instructor. Studying with a private instructor one-on-one is the ultimate way to make rapid progress on the guitar, although it is more expensive than classes. A good guitar instructor can show you things in a matter of weeks that it might take you a year to figure out on your own. It's important that you

ELSEWHERE ON THE WEB

▶ If you want to do some research on music schools in your area—or anywhere else in the country—here's a resource for connecting with music colleges in the United States. The site allows you to search for music schools, colleges, and universities by state. Just go to www .a2zcolleges.com/music/ index.html.

trust your instructor and that you admire his or her ability on the guitar for this relationship to work, so if after a few weeks you're not getting that feeling from the first one you choose, look for a new one.

Try music school for the complete experience. Music school (college for musicians) is generally a place where you immerse yourself for four years or so in the foundations of music theory, harmony, composition, and performance, majoring in your instrument or the musical pursuit that most interests you. When you graduate you'll have the foundation you need to pursue any number of careers in music.

Get Linked

You can find information about subjects above and beyond what we've had time to discuss in these chapters on my **About.com** *site. As you continue on guitar you may well have the desire to express your creativity by writing your own songs. Whether you're experienced at songwriting or not, this series of lessons about writing better songs has something to teach you. Check out this interesting link.*

WRITING BETTER SONGS   Series of lessons about songwriting
http://about.com/guitar/songwriting

Appendices

You've reached the end of the book, and you're well on your way to becoming a skilled acoustic guitarist. Even though you've absorbed a ton of new information and learned lots of new skills, chances are you still have a lingering question or two. Well, the following three appendices have got you covered. Appendix A is a glossary of guitar and music terms that appear in red throughout the book. The alphabetized glossary makes it easy to find the definitions whenever you need them. Appendix B is a list of helpful Web sites that offer more information on the topics covered in the book, such as guitar history and careers in music. Finally, Appendix C is a list of books and albums that might interest you as a newly minted guitarist.

Appendix A

Glossary

½ size

The smallest standard guitar size, measuring approximately 34" from headstock to the far end of the body, as opposed to about 40" for a full size guitar.

¾ size

The middle standard guitar size, measuring approximately 36" from headstock to the far end of the body, as opposed to about 40" for a full size guitar.

6-string classical

An acoustic guitar strung with six nylon strings.

6-string steel

An acoustic guitar strung with six steel strings.

69 chord

A major or minor chord that also contains the 6th and 9th notes of the major scale it is based on.

8-bar blues

A blues progression comprised of 8 bars each containing four beats. Bar 1 is the root chord, bar 2 is the 5th chord, bars 3-4 are the 4th chord, bar 5 is the root chord, bar 6 is the 5th chord, bar 7 is the root chord, and bar 8 is the fifth chord.

12-bar blues

A standard blues progression comprised of 12 bars each containing four beats. Bars 1-4 are the root chord, bars 5-6 are the 4th chord, bars 7-8 are the root chord, bars 9-10 are the 5th chord (or the 10th bar might be the 4th chord), bar 11 is the root chord, and bar 12 is the 5th chord.

12-string

An acoustic guitar, usually strung with steel strings, which uses two strings where each string would normally be. The pairs of strings are tuned an octave apart or to exactly the same pitch, to double the sound of each string.

16-bar blues

A blues progression comprised of 16 bars each containing 4 beats. There are several variations of this progression.

accent

A single note picked or a chord strummed harder than the notes or chords surrounding it for emphasis.

acoustic/electric

An acoustic guitar that has a pickup built in so that it can be amplified without using a microphone.

action

The height of the strings above the fingerboard.

alternate bass strum

A strumming pattern that alternates single bass notes with strumming to create a "bass line" under the chord progression.

alternate picking

Playing notes one at a time with a pick, alternating between downstrokes and upstrokes.

alternate tunings

Changing the tuning of one or more strings of the guitar to deviate from the standard E A D G B E tuning. In most cases the strings are tuned to form an open chord.

anchor

To rest a finger (usually the fourth finger) of the picking hand on the top of the guitar for stability of position. Generally used for fingerpicking.

arpeggio

The notes of a chord played one at a time.

ascending scale

A scale in which the notes are going up in pitch.

attack

The degree of force with which strings are strummed, picked, or fingerpicked.

back

The large surface of the guitar body parallel to the top.

bar

Another word for measure.

barre

> Using one finger on the fretting hand to play more than one string at a time.

barre chord

> A chord played with closed left hand fingering with no open or unfretted strings, with the first finger barring all or most of the strings. A barre chord is a movable chord.

bass line

> A series of notes played at low pitches, usually to accompany other parts being played at higher pitches on the guitar or by other instruments.

beats per second (BPS)

> The number of cycles, or beats, at which a note vibrates in one second.

bend

> To stretch one or more strings across the fingerboard in order to raise the pitch of the note.

bend and release

> A string bend where the note is bent up and then returned to its original pitch.

blues scale

> A minor pentatonic scale with an extra note added between the third and fourth notes of the scale.

body

> The largest part of the instrument, the body is comprised of the top, sides, and back, as well as interior bracing. When the strings are vibrating the body becomes a resonating cavity that amplifies the sound and projects it forward through the sound hole.

bridge

> A piece of material (generally wood) attached to the top of the guitar that is used to hold the strings in place. The bridge (in conjunction with the saddle) transfers the string vibrations into the soundboard.

bridge pin

> A small removable peg (usually made of plastic) that fits into a hole in the bridge of an acoustic guitar. One peg holds each string in place.

chord

> Two or more notes played at the same time.

chord progression

> Two or more chords that repeat in the same order in a song or other piece of music.

chromatic scale

> A scale that includes all 12 notes in an octave.

chromatic tuner

> An electronic device that "listens" to the pitch of each string, tells you what note it is, and then advises you with a visual display (either a needle on a real or virtual meter, or a light

display) that you need to tune the string higher or lower to get it in perfect tune.

closed left hand fingering

A fingering pattern that includes no open or unfretted strings.

cycles per second

Sound is actually physical waves being pushed through the air, and the number of waves, or cycles, per second is how different pitches are measured. The open A string on the guitar is 110 cycles per second, making each wave 1/110 of a second.

DADGAD tuning

An alternate tuning that changes the strings to D A D G A D.

descending scale

A scale in which the notes are going down in pitch.

diagram

A visual illustration that indicates the strings of the guitar and where to place your fingers, such as a chord diagram or the tab staff.

diatonic chords

The chords based on one scale that can be built using only the notes of that scale.

dominant seventh chord

A chord built of the root, third, fifth, and flatted seventh notes of the major scale it's based on.

downstroke

Picking or strumming strings with a downward motion, in the direction of the floor.

dreadnought

A very popular acoustic guitar body shape, the dreadnought is rather large and typically emphasizes the bass frequencies of the instrument. The dreadnought shape was originally introduced by Martin Guitars, and is named after the British battleship *H.M.S. Dreadnought.*

drone

A continuous note or notes that accompany a chord progression and/or melody, generally in the bass register. A single drone note is also referred to as a "pedal" or "pedal note," a reference to the way bass drones are played on the organ with a foot pedal.

Drop D tuning

An alternate tuning that changes the strings to D A D G B E.

face

Another word for top.

fifth chord

Another name for power chord.

fingerboard

The flat face of the neck of the guitar, onto which the metallic frets are placed.

fingerpicking
> To use the thumb and the first three fingers (sometimes the fourth one gets into the act, too) of the picking hand to pluck the strings individually, either all at once or in "arpeggiated rhythms," which means the strings are plucked in rhythmic sequences.

first inversion
> A chord voicing where the root note has been shifted to the highest note being played.

flat (♭)
> A note one half step lower.

folk guitar
> Another name for the 6-string steel guitar.

frequency
> The number of beats per second at which a note vibrates.

fret
> (1) Strip of material found on the fingerboard, typically made of nickel-silver, that comes into contact with a depressed string and creates a pitch when that string is plucked. (2) The space on the fingerboard between two frets (or a fret and the nut) where you place your finger to play a note. The space on the headstock side of the metal fret is the corresponding fret space.

fretboard
> Another word for fingerboard.

fretting hand

The primary hand used to press the strings against the fingerboard.

guitar riff

A series of notes played on the guitar.

guitar tablature

A graphic way of displaying music for guitarists that displays the six strings of the instrument and indicates with numbers on each string which frets should be played.

half step

The smallest interval in Western music, two adjacent notes.

hammer-on

Generating a note by bringing your fingertip down firmly onto the fret and holding it down while the note rings, without the use of a pick.

harmonic

A little bell tone produced on certain frets of the guitar by lightly touching the string directly above the fret and then lifting your finger off the string at the same time that you pluck the string. Harmonic frets on the guitar include the 5th, 7th, and 12th frets.

headstock

The piece at the end of the neck that holds the tuning machines.

heel

    The heel of the neck is the part of the neck that attaches to the body of the guitar.

inlays

    Round dots (or other shapes) used to mark your position on the neck as you play. There are inlays for the same purpose set into the upper edge of the fingerboard.

interval

    The space between two notes.

intonation

    The degree of pitch accuracy relative to correct standard pitch. On guitar good intonation means that the fretted notes are in tune all the way up and down the neck.

inversion

    Playing the notes of a chord in a different order to create the same chord with a different voicing.

lead

    Another word for playing a solo, or for occupying that role in a band, also called "lead guitar."

lead guitar

    Playing a solo on guitar, or occupying the role of guitar soloist in a band.

leading bass strum

    A strumming pattern that uses a single bass note to lead into the strumming that follows for the rest of the pattern.

left-handed guitar

An instrument set up for left-handed players, with the strings in reverse order and the pick guard and cutaway (if present) on the opposite side of the neck.

lick

Another word for riff or phrase.

Low C tuning

An alternate tuning that changes the strings to C G D G A D.

major chord

A chord made up of three notes: the root, major third, and fifth.

major scale

A scale formed of the following intervals: whole step, whole step, half step, whole step, whole step, whole step, half step.

major second

An interval where the higher note is two half steps higher than the lower note.

major seventh chord

A chord built of the root, third, fifth, and seventh notes of the major scale it's based on.

major third

An interval where the higher note is four half steps higher than the lower note.

mastering

A step in the recording process, after mixing is complete, where the overall sound of the piece is polished.

measure

One group of the number of beats allowed by the "time signature" of a song or other piece of music. Time signatures are written as fractions, such as 4/4. The top number tells you the number of beats in a measure, and the bottom number tells you what kind of note gets one beat. In the case of 4/4 time (the most commonly used time signature) there are four beats in every measure, and the quarter note gets one beat. In standard notation or on chord charts a vertical line is drawn every time the number of beats allowed in a measure have been used up, and the space between every two lines is one measure. In 4/4 time, every time four beats go by a new measure begins.

metronome

A device that emits a steady click at a speed that you can set and vary. Used to practice playing steadily in time.

minor chord

A chord made up of three notes: the root, minor third, and fifth.

minor seventh chord

A chord built of the root, flatted third, fifth, and flatted seventh notes of the major scale it's based on.

minor third

An interval where the higher note is three half steps higher than the lower note.

mixing

A process used in recording where all of the instruments are blended together so that their relationship to each other is ideal.

mode

One of a series of scales that grew out of ancient Greek music. Modes are centered around a C major scale, and each of the seven modes uses the same consecutive notes of that C major scale—but each mode begins on a different note of the scale.

movable chord

A chord played with closed left hand fingering, with no open or unfretted strings, so that it can be played in any key using the same fingering simply by moving the chord up and down the neck.

movable scale

A scale played with closed left hand fingering, so that it can be played in any key using the same fingering simply by moving the scale up and down the neck.

Nashville tuning

An alternate tuning where the notes E A D G B E are maintained, but the sixth through third strings are replaced with alternate strings and tuned one octave higher.

nato

A type of wood closely related to mahogany that is known for its resonance and is often used to build guitars, usually for the neck, sides, and/or back.

neck

The long piece of the guitar between the headstock and the body.

nut

A little block made out of plastic, bone, composite, or metal between the neck and the headstock that has six small grooves cut into it to guide the strings up to the tuning machines.

nylon-string

Another name for the 6-string classical guitar.

octave

An interval where the higher note is 12 half steps higher than the lower note.

open position

The hand position at the bottom of the neck that incorporates open strings into the chord or scale being played.

Open C tuning

An alternate tuning that changes the strings to C G C G C E.

Open D tuning

An alternate tuning that changes the strings to D A D F♯ A D.

Open G tuning

An alternate tuning that changes the strings to D G D G B D.

open tunings

Another term for alternate tunings.

palm muting

A guitar technique executed by the picking hand where the base of the palm is used to muffle the strings slightly while they are plucked with the pick.

passing notes

Notes that aren't in a particular scale but are used to ease the passage between one scale note and the next.

pentatonic scale

A scale with five notes per octave.

phrase

A series of notes grouped together to express a musical idea.

phrasing

Expressing musical ideas through short groups of notes that have a discernable beginning, middle, and an end that resolves. A phrase in music performs a function similar to that of a sentence in language.

pick guard

A piece of plastic glued to the top just below the sound hole. Just as it sounds, this is designed to protect the top of the instrument from damage inflicted by the pick.

picking

The act of striking the string with a pick, causing the string to vibrate.

picking hand

The hand used to strike the strings of the instrument, whether by strumming, picking, or fingerpicking.

pitch

The degree to which a note is high or low as determined by the frequency of the vibration of sound waves the note produces. The higher the note, the higher frequency it produces.

pluck

To strike the string with a pick or finger in order to make it vibrate.

polyrhythm

Two or more rhythmic patterns played at the same time.

position shift

To move the position of the hand to a different location up or down the neck.

power chord

A chord made up of two notes, the root and the fifth.

pre-bend

A string bend where the string is muted during the bend up so that you only hear the note as it's returning from the top of the bend to the original note.

pull-off

Generating a note by pulling a fingertip off of the fret and holding the note you're fingering below it down while that note rings, without the use of a pick.

punch-in

A method used in recording to begin and end recording in the middle of a previously recorded track in order to correct a mistake.

real pitch

The pitches of notes that correspond to standard orchestral pitch, which is defined as the A above middle C on the piano being set at 440 cycles per second.

reference pitch

A pitch from a source other than your instrument, such as a piano, another guitar, or a tuning fork, used to tune your instrument.

resonator guitar

An acoustic guitar that has a metal resonator built into the body, a system originally invented to make guitars louder. The bridge of the instrument is connected directly to the resonator, which when vibrating acts like a speaker cone and makes the sound louder, with a tone that's almost banjo-like.

rhythm guitar

Playing chords in a rhythmic pattern on guitar, or occupying the role of the chording guitarist in a band.

riff

A series of notes played on any instrument.

root

The first note of the scale the key of a chord or piece of music is based on.

root position

A chord voicing where the root note is the lowest note being played.

saddle

A hard, thin piece of plastic, bone, or composite mounted on the bridge that the strings pass over between the nut and the bridge pins. The vibration of the strings is transferred into the body of the guitar via the saddle and the bridge.

scale

A series of notes that reach from one octave to the next octave, and repeat in the same order as the scale moves from octave to octave.

second inversion

A chord voicing where the second note is the highest note being played, and the root note is the second highest.

semitone

A half step.

seven chord

Another name for seventh chord.

seventh chord

Any chord built of the root, third, fifth, and seventh notes of the major scale it's built on.

sharp (♯)

A note one half step higher.

sides

The narrow pieces of the body between the front and the back.

sight-reading

The ability to look at a written page of music and play the music immediately.

single-note melody

A series of notes played one at a time.

slash chord

A chord with a specific note added that is voiced below the rest of the notes in the chord.

slide

(1) A fingering technique where one finger slides up or down a string while pressing against the frets to create multiple notes. (2) A smooth tube, generally made of glass, chrome, steel, or brass, that is worn over a finger on the fretting hand and used to slide up and down the strings without pressing against the frets to create a slippery sound that includes all pitches between one note and the next without being limited to half steps.

solo

(1) Playing solo means performing without the accompaniment of any other musicians. (2) Playing a solo means playing the featured instrument while being accompanied by other musicians.

sonokelin

A hard wood often used to build guitars, usually for the fingerboard and/or saddle.

sound hole

The round hole in the center of the top of a guitar, from which the sound emanates.

standard notation

Music written on the standard 5-line staff using notes.

strap button

A small knob attached to the body of the guitar where the sides meet at the bottom which is used to attach a guitar strap to the instrument. Some acoustic guitars have a second strap button mounted on the heel of the neck.

string bend

A string bend where the note is bent up and then the string is muted at the top of the bend so you don't hear the string returning to its original pitch.

string bending

A guitar technique in which the pitch of a note is raised, by stretching the string across the fingerboard, in either a downward or upward motion.

strings

Long pieces of metal or nylon stretched between the tuning machine shaft and the bridge that vibrate when struck to produce the sound of the instrument. Steel strings are wire manufactured to exact gauges and made of various composites of steel, nickel, bronze, and copper. The lower-pitch strings are wound with a wrapping of steel, nickel, or bronze. Nylon strings feel like plastic. The lower-pitched strings are also wound with metal wrapping.

strumming

The act of brushing the pick (or empty hand) across several strings at once, causing the strings to vibrate.

strumming pattern with bass line

A strumming pattern that incorporates a series of single bass notes between the strumming to create a "bass line" under the chord progression.

sus4 chord

A chord built of the first, fourth, and fifth notes of the major scale on which it's based.

tab

Abbreviation of "guitar tablature."

tab staff

A special staff used for guitar tablature that has six lines, each of which indicates a string on the instrument.

tempo

The speed at which music is played.

tone

(1) Another word for whole tone. (2) The timbre or character of the sound being produced by an instrument.

top

The surface of the body that lies just below the strings, which supports the bridge and contains the sound hole.

tuners

Another name for tuning machines.

tuning fork

A piece of metal shaped like a wishbone that vibrates at a pre-determined frequency when struck and produces a reference pitch for tuning. The most common pitch of a tuning fork is A 440, which is the A that vibrates at 440 cycles per second.

tuning head

Another name for the headstock.

tuning machines

The machines on the headstock used to adjust the pitch of the strings.

turnaround

A phrase, or "fill" played in the last two bars of a blues progression to lead back into the beginning of the progression.

upstroke

Picking or strumming strings with an upward motion, away from the floor.

uptempo

A fast or faster speed at which a melody or chord progression is being played.

vamp

A situation where the chord progression lingers on one chord for a long time.

vibrato

A wavering effect applied to the pitch of a note. On guitar vibrato is achieved by repeatedly stretching and relaxing the string in a rhythmic manner.

voice leading

The process of each note of a chord moving smoothly and minimally to the next chord, achieved by playing the notes of the two voicings as close together as possible while playing them on the same string group.

voicing

The order (from low to high pitch) that the notes of a chord are played. The same notes can be arranged in several different ways and they will still be the same chord, but each voicing will sound different.

whole step

An interval where the higher note is two half steps higher than the lower note.

whole tone

A whole step.

Other Sites

About.com Blues Site

Interesting Web site by John Babich, with blues history, lessons, and information about the current blues scene.

http://blues.about.com

Acoustic Fingerstyle Guitar Page

Paul Kucharski's comprehensive fingerpicking page with articles, open tunings, tips, and even guitar jokes.

www.acousticfingerstyle.com

Acoustic Guitar Magazine

This monthly covers the acoustic guitar scene, including artists, instrument reviews, and lessons.

www.acousticguitar.com/index.asp

Archive of Misheard Lyrics

Hysterically funny Web site where people share what they think are the lyrics to their favorite songs.

www.kissthisguy.com

Bluegrass Guitar Home Page

Steve Carr's bluegrass site with history, artist profiles, lessons, and links.

www.bluegrassguitar.com

Brazilian Guitar Page

Joe Carter's interesting page on important Brazilian musicians featuring many guitarists. Includes photos and audio clips.

www.joecartermusic.com/brasilian.html

Classical and Flamenco Guitar

John Philip Dimick's site covers classical and flamenco guitar styles and includes beginner pages for each.

www.guitarist.com

Find a Guitar Teacher

This instruction page at Wholenote.com connects you with guitar teachers in your area.

www.wholenote.com/teachers/browse.asp

Flatpicking Guitar Magazine

Features lessons, links, and information about the world of flat-picking guitar.

www.flatpick.com

Frets.com Acoustic Guitar Owner's Manual

The Frets.com information center has a lot of good information on caring for your guitar. Note that some processes described on this site should only be done by professionals.

www.frets.com/FRETSPages/OwnerManual/manssguitar.html

Guitar Show Calendar

Guide to guitar shows throughout the year.

www.guitarshowcalendar.com

Harmony Central Guitar Review Database

A clearinghouse for people's opinions about any guitar you might be interested in or considering buying.

www.harmony-central.com/Guitar/Data4

History of the Blues

Brief history of the blues with great photos, including Robert Johnson's famous crossroads location in Mississippi.

www.history-of-rock.com/blues.htm

Jazz Guitar

Bob Patterson's jazz guitar site has feature articles, lessons, and links to jazz Web sites.

www.jazzguitar.com

Music and Guitar Associations

List of music and guitar associations with active links to each of them.

www.guitarfox.com/guitarassociations.htm

Music Degrees and Rock Guitarists

An essay about what musicians may gain from pursuing higher education.

www.guitar9.com/columnist394.html

Music Industry Jobs and Careers in Music

Information about jobs and careers, including interviews of people who have made it in various positions in the industry.

http://about.com/musicians/musiccareers

Online Guitar Magazines

List of online guitar magazines with active links to each of them.

www.guitarfox.com/guitarmagazines.htm

Planet Dobro

Carl Weingarten's far-reaching site covers the world of slide guitar.

www.mphase.com/planetd2.htm

Vintage Fender Guitars, Amps, Basses Information

Information about vintage Fender equipment, including the company's line of acoustic guitars.

www.provide.net/~cfh/fender.html

Appendix C

Further Reading and Listening

Reading

Acoustic Guitar Slide Basics by David Hamburger

> Excellent beginner book for playing slide guitar with lessons on technique, open tunings, guides to equipment, and an accompanying CD.

Acoustic Guitars: The Illustrated Encyclopedia by Dave Hunter, et. al.

> A comprehensive guide to acoustic guitars with photos and great information.

Beginning Fingerstyle Guitar by Lou Manzi

> Learn fingerpicking from the ground up with one of the masters of the form.

How to Play Blues Guitar: The Basics and Beyond by Richard Johnston (Ed.)

> All the techniques and tunings you need to get started playing blues from top experts.

The Ultimate Guitar Chord Big Book: Over 100,000 Chords by Don Latarski

> The title says it all. Excellent reference for looking up chords you need or experimenting with new ones.

Listening

Aerial Boundaries, Michael Hedges

> Ethereal guitar compositions played with Hedges's signature multi-attack style.

Akata Meso, D'Gary

> Madagascar guitarist D'Gary spotlights his unpredictable finger-style and unique approach to open tunings on this album.

The Best Of Doc Watson 1964–1968, Doc Watson

> The nitro-fueled flatpicker is in great form on this "best of" collection recorded between 1964 and 1968.

Blue Country Heart, Jorma Kaukonen

> Former Jefferson Airplane guitarist goes back to his acoustic blues roots on this fine album of country blues classics.

Chautauqua, Pat Metheny

> Top jazz guitarist Metheny in a revealing solo acoustic guitar setting with layered tracks, recorded in 1979.

Dancing in the Dragon's Jaws, Bruce Cockburn

> The Canadian folkie brings his strong songwriting and sparkling open-tuned guitar playing to this acoustic album from 1979.

Flesh on Flesh, Al DiMeola
DiMeola exercises his awesome chops on both electric and acoustic guitars in a group setting.

Grisman & Garcia, Jerry Garcia and David Grisman
The venerable Grateful Dead guitarist Garcia and mandolin ace Grisman team up on this sparkling acoustic pick-fest.

Highlights from the Julian Bream Edition, Julian Bream
One of the top classical guitarists of our time, in both solo and orchestral settings.

King of the Delta Blues, Robert Johnson
Sixteen songs by the legendary blues pioneer, recorded in the 1930s.

Knuckle Down, Ani DiFranco
The latest album by this acoustic powerhouse finds her at the top of her game.

The Legendary Segovia, Andrés Segovia
These recordings were made between 1927 and 1939 and capture Segovia as a fiery young guitar virtuoso.

Legs to Make Us Longer, Kaki King
King is a force of nature on acoustic guitar, and her percussive style and creative use of open tunings make this album a signpost for the new direction of the instrument.

One Guitar No Vocals, Leo Kottke
This solo guitar setting provides a perfect opportunity to study this 12-string fingerpicking master's mesmerizing technique.

Quintette du Hot Club de France: 25 Classics 1934–1940, Django Reinhardt

This disc captures the frantic energy of this swinging band, which captivated Paris in the 1930s.

Requia & Other Compositions for Guitar Solo, John Fahey

Fahey is at the height of his powers on this album as he weaves his "cerebral symphonies."

Robot Monster, Don Ross

Ross displays his rhythmic, percussive, and swinging guitar style on this infectious solo guitar album.

Solo, Badi Assad

The Brazilian classical guitar master unleashes her fiery instrumental style on her debut album.

Song to a Seagull, Joni Mitchell

Her debut album from 1968 showcases her magnificent guitar style and composition.

Theme to the Guardian, Bill Connors

Former Return to Forever guitarist showcases his masterful composition and spellbinding technique on this solo guitar album.

Thieves and Poets, John McLaughlin

Mahavishnu Orchestra firebrand guitarist McLaughlin playing acoustic in solo and orchestral settings.

Today, Mississippi John Hurt

This album, recorded in 1966, is widely considered one of the best by this Delta blues legend.

The *Ultimate Guitar Album*, John Williams

The classical guitar genius shines in both solo and orchestral settings on this collection album.

The *Water Garden*, Alex DeGrassi

DeGrassi demonstrates his phenomenal fingerstyle technique and use of open tunings on this solo acoustic album.

INDEX

Practicing. *See also* specific topics
  barre chords, 106–7, 123, 136, 159
  blues scale, 68, 122, 136
  chords/scales, 37–38, 49–50, 68, 80, 106–7, 174, 196–97
  enjoyment and, 68–69
  fingerpicking, 123, 137, 159, 174, 197
  F major chord, 80
  hammer-ons/pull-offs, 123, 196
  importance of, 37, 49, 50, 67–69, 79, 80–81, 196
  major chord inversions, 174–76
  making weaknesses strengths, 91
  with metronome. See Metronomes
  minor chord inversions, 197
  power chords, 80, 107
  seventh chords, 107, 197
  slash chords, 137
  slides, 136, 159, 196
  string bends, 137, 159, 174, 197
  sus4 chords, 159
Private lessons, 231–32
Pull-offs, 118–19, 123, 196

R
Reading music (sight-reading), 86, 229–30
Real pitch, 29
Recording artists, 227–28

Reinhardt, Django, 222, 268
Renting guitars, 1
Repairs, 217–18, 219. *See also* Maintaining guitars
Resonator guitars
  described, 3
  music type and, 3–4
  recommended model, 8
Resources (additional)
  books, 231, 265–66
  classes, 231
  DVDs, 229
  listening, 265–69
  other Web sites, 261–64
Rhythm guitar, 31
Right hand position, 21–23
Robertson, Robbie, 133
Root notes, 74
Root position, 166, 183

S
Saddle, 19
Scales. *See also* Practicing
  ascending, 33
  benefits of, 57
  blues, 53–57, 88–90
  chromatic, 31–32, 97–99
  descending, 33
  Dorian mode and, 145–48
  harmonic minor, 124
  introduction to, 31–33
  modes and. See Modes
  movable, 54, 97–99, 140

  pentatonic, 55–57
  Phrygian Dominant, 148–52
  playing in multiple keys, 54, 139–40
  reading diagrams for, 31–32
  tips for improving, 33
  two-octave, 139–40
Second inversion, 167, 184
Segovia, Andrés, 222, 225, 267
Seventh barre chords
  dominant, 151, 180–82
  introduction to, 179–82
  major, 179–80
  minor, 181–82
Seventh chords, 84–86, 107, 197
Sharps/flats, 83–84
Sight-reading, 86, 229–30
Single-note melodies, 22, 31
6-string classical (nylon-string) guitars
  described, 2
  music type and, 3–4
  recommended models, 7
6-string steel (folk) guitars
  described, 2
  music type and, 3–4
  recommended models, 4–6
  3/4 size models, 6–7
16-bar blues, 58, 59
Slash chords, 129–31, 136, 173
Slides, 13–14, 104, 131, 132–33, 136, 159, 196
Solos
  improvising lesson, 93
  lead guitar and, 22, 31

Tuning, 28–31
    after changing strings, 210
    alternate (open), 101–4, 119–20
    DADGAD, 102–3
    Drop D, 101–2
    electronic tuner for, 13, 29
    first string, then other five,
      28–30
    guitar to itself, 29
    Nashville, 121
    Open C, 119–20
    Open D, 103
    Open G, 104
    staying in tune and, 10
    training ear/voice to pitches,
      30–31
    using referencing pitch, 28–29
Tuning forks, 28
Tuning head, 18
Tuning machines (tuners)
    changing strings and, 206–9,
      211
    feel of, 10
    purpose of, 18
    replacing, 218
Turnaround, 59
12-string steel guitars
    described, 2
    music type and, 3–4
    recommended models, 7
12-bar blues, 53, 57–58, 59, 63,
    64, 65, 67
2-bar strumming, 193–95
Two-octave scales, 139–40,
    142–43

U

Upstrokes, introduced, 22. *See
    also* Strumming

V

Vamps, 143, 148, 151
Voice leading, 183, 188
Voicings, 109–10, 166

W

Warming up, importance of, 82
Watson, Doc, 226, 266
Williams, John, 225, 269
Writing songs, 150, 228, 233